TRANSFORM PRESSURE TO POWER

8 MINDSET STRATEGIES TO ACHIEVE EVENTING SUCCESS

HELEN RENNIE

First edition published by Helen Rennie

www.TransformPressureToPower.com

ISBN-13: 978-1518610509

Contents

Testimonials

"As a result of performance coaching, I've improved my show jumping performance at competitions and after stepping up to Novice level, I've achieved several double clears which has enabled me to qualify for my first 1* event at Osberton. It has completely changed my performance and competition results for the better because the techniques I've learnt have helped me ride to the best of my ability. These techniques have proven to be so valuable that I will be using them in the rest of my competing career."

Rebecca Page - Eventing

"Performance coaching has proven to be a great success in helping me progress within eventing and as a rider in general. Before my sessions I was quick to become stressed and nervous before competitions, to the point where it would take over my state of mind. Performance coaching has helped me recognise early stages of nerves so I can effectively deal with and control my state of mind. This has had a positive effect on my riding at competitions; firstly, it is a more relaxing experience and, secondly, there has been a particular improvement in results, especially in dressage, and we have even moved up a level. Being able to control the way I think and my state of mind has given me the confidence to aim higher and move my horse through the levels and actually believe in myself to do it! I would like to say a big thank you to Helen who has helped me greatly in achieving a positive and successful state of mind!"

Charlotte Huband - Eventing

"Helen has helped dramatically improve my ability to maintain focus in all three phases by being able to control any negative thoughts I have throughout the day, to create a more optimistic thought pattern. I have seen a difference in the way I think at events in a short space of time, and just starting with a more positive outlook trickles down to how I perform or how I analyse when things haven't gone the right way."
Izzy Squire - Eventing

"I found the mindset techniques that Helen gave me extremely useful and helped me to maintain my focus throughout the cross country phase at a recent event which meant we went clear! I also used the techniques to help me deal with a couple of challenges we had on the day which meant I was able to keep calm and quickly refocus so I could perform well."
Elaine - Event Rider, Scotland

About the Author

Helen specialises in working with competition riders of all ages and skill levels to strengthen their mental game and improve their performance and competition results. Helen's mission is to effectively unlock riders' performance potential so they can perform at their very best and achieve the results they want.

Through Helen's effective Transform Pressure to Power™ coaching methods and book, she is committed to enabling riders to learn the techniques and mindset needed for success in eventing. Helen assesses the needs of each rider she works with, tailors the techniques and provides the tools that will give the rider everything they need to improve their performance and ultimately achieve greater success.

Helen's book, Transform Pressure to Power™, is the first of its kind to be written specifically for event riders. Each of the strategies has been adapted to the exact requirements of equestrian sport and has been written with the busy event rider in mind. In this book, you'll discover Helen's innovative methods and the exact tools you need to improve your performance and ultimately achieve greater success. You can read the book cover-to-cover or use it strategically to address specific problems, one at a time.

As an author, successful Equestrian Performance Coach and the founder of Altair Performance Coaching Ltd, Helen has created a set of proven mindset strategies designed to unlock an equestrian athlete's performance potential. Helen is a Licensed Master Practitioner of NLP™, personally trained and certified by the co-creator of NLP™, Richard Bandler and Society of NLP™. She is also qualified in Sports Psychology and has a Masters degree in Human Sciences from University of Oxford. In her spare time she loves to ride, having ridden and owned horses for a number of years, and is a passionate supporter of British Eventing.

Foreword

Helen's *Transform Pressure To PowerTM* method is an incredible, extraordinary set of strategies that really do work, and are guaranteed to improve your performance. If you are an event rider with ambitions to elevate your performance and achieve fantastic results, you are exactly in the right place.

Helen is an amazing coach with a deep understanding of what it takes to develop a winning mindset, and her techniques are the perfect complement to your technical training. Her results and testimonials speak for themselves.

Helen is an inspiring person to work with because of her belief that everyone has untapped potential and is capable of achieving amazing results. She is 100% focused on identifying the quickest possible route from problem to solution, and helping you to make lasting changes.

Even reading just one chapter of this book will change the way you think and the way you perform at competitions forever. The strategies that Helen shares with you in this book are incredibly powerful. To get maximum value, please make sure you complete the actions she gives you in each of these chapters. She really does want you to see you succeed and perform at your best, which is why this book has been designed as a practical, problem-solving guide that will help you make lasting improvements to your performance at competitions.

Think of this book as a coaching session with Helen. She's here to help you every step of the way, so just follow each step and you'll be amazed at the results you achieve. Pay careful attention to each of the strategies that Helen shares with you in this book. Your eventing career depends on it.

Raymond Aaron
New York Times Best-Selling Author
www.2dayTycoon.com

(Raymond is the author of Branding Small Business for Dummies and Double Your Income Doing What You Love, besides many other bestselling books. He is known as the #1 success and investment coach, teaching people just like you how to use his goal setting strategies to change your life.)

Dedication

This book is dedicated to you, the reader of this book. I know you have chosen this book because you want to improve your performance and results at competitions, and I know that the strategies in this book are going to help you. They helped me overcome a serious setback, and I use these strategies to this day to help me achieve my dreams, one of which is writing this book and getting it published!

I wanted to write this book because I passionately believe that all riders should have access to these mindset strategies, no matter what their goals and ambitions. I hope that you will use these strategies to help you achieve the success you truly desire and get greater enjoyment and learning from each and every competition.

Stay calm and focused under pressure!

Best wishes
Helen

Acknowledgements

I want to thank Raymond Aaron for his incredible support and encouragement. I also want to thank Vishal Morjaria for his inspiration and enthusiasm which has helped me every step of the way in navigating the path to publishing my book.

Massive thanks to the wonderful international event riders who took time out of their hectic schedules to share their valuable insights with me – Olivia Wilmot, Elspeth Jamieson, Camilla Kruger and Daniel Scott.

I also want to thank my husband Jonathan, my Mum, Dad and Gran, all of whom have supported me unconditionally throughout the book writing process and have always believed in me and helped me through moments of self-doubt throughout my life.

Thanks also to Peter Haynes, master coach and 1998 Australian International 3 Day Event Champion, for his awesome inspiration which helped me rebuild my confidence after my riding accident and showed me that my dream job was somewhere outside the corporate world.

Finally, this book is in memory of my amazing first horse Floyd, who was an incredible schoolmaster and a once in a lifetime horse. Although he is gone, he will never be forgotten.

Note to the Reader

The information, including opinion and analysis, contained herein is based on the author's personal experiences and is not intended to provide professional advice.

The author and the publisher make no warranties, either expressed or implied, concerning the accuracy, applicability, effectiveness, reliability or suitability of the contents. If you wish to apply or follow the advice or recommendations mentioned herein, you take full responsibility for your actions. The author and publisher of this book shall in no event be held liable for any direct, indirect, incidental or consequential damages arising directly or indirectly from the use of any of the information contained in this book.

All content is for information only and is not warranted for content accuracy or any other implied or explicit purpose.

WHY MINDSET MATTERS

WHERE IT STARTED

I don't remember much about my accident. I remember being catapulted out of the saddle and being suspended mid-air for what felt like a very long time. I remember thinking "this is going to hurt." That's it. I'm told I was unconscious for several minutes and that when I came round I said "Where is he?" (my horse) and "I'm getting back on." By the time I came round my horse had been returned to his stable and the yard owner had called an ambulance. My concussion meant that I didn't really process what had happened for a while. Even whilst we were waiting for the ambulance, I remember thinking that everyone was making a fuss and that an ambulance was completely unnecessary. That is until I was loaded into the back of the ambulance on a stretcher and in a neck brace. Shock finally set in. I suddenly felt so cold, I struggled to breathe. Thankfully this only lasted a short while and, once it had passed, denial set in.

So when I got to the hospital and the doctor told me she was certain I had broken my neck, I told her that was impossible. Maintaining my stance that everyone was making a big fuss out of nothing, I spent the next 6 hours in a head and neck brace, unable to do anything other than look at the ceiling, whilst I was sent for an X-ray and a CT scan. After the X-ray I began to feel more confident in my self-diagnosis that I was perfectly fine because the doctor told me that the X-ray had not shown a fracture. She then quickly said "but the swelling around your neck is very serious so I'm sending you for a CT scan to confirm the fracture." She was totally convinced I'd broken it. So it was a huge relief when the CT scan confirmed that, in fact, my neck was completely intact. I was diagnosed with severe whiplash, sent home with painkillers and told to rest.

I left the hospital feeling tired but happy. I convinced myself that everything would return to normal and I'd be back riding again very soon. That was my first mistake. Returning to normal was extremely difficult because my severe whiplash (that I thought would just be a bit uncomfortable) was very painful and I lost movement in my neck. I became unable to turn my neck much, which meant my neck and shoulders became very stiff. It took 18 months for me to regain movement in my neck and even now, 4 years on, it still occasionally hurts and I still don't have full range of movement.

My second mistake was returning to riding my crazy horse. In fact it took another 18 months of working with him for me to abandon riding him. Instead of rebuilding my confidence after my accident, I simply kept putting it to the test over and over again. Sometimes I regret my decision to keep riding him after the accident. But it is the reason I am here today, writing this book and helping riders to build a strong mindset for competitions to improve their performance and results.

Following my accident, an interesting psychological paradox emerged in my behaviour. Having studied Human Sciences at Oxford University I became both fascinated and frustrated in equal measure by this paradox. Because my horse would do almost anything to get me off (buck, rear, spin, bolt), I had to become a better rider to stay on, so I developed a much deeper seat. You would think that this would have improved my confidence but it didn't. My confidence plummeted. Riding was no longer something I enjoyed or got a buzz from; it was just plain scary. So the paradox was that my skill level had improved whilst my mindset had deteriorated which meant there was a big gap between my mindset and my skills.

I knew that, if my mindset was as strong as my skill level, I would be capable of doing pretty much anything with my riding, so I was determined to find ways to improve my confidence and get back to feeling great in the saddle. In the time since my accident I have found new and different ways to rebuild my confidence and it has meant that I have discovered some really powerful techniques. So when I became inspired to set up my coaching practise for competition riders, I chose to work with world-class leaders in NLP (Dr Richard Bandler) and coaching (Curly Martin) to really understand these techniques. In developing my own method, Transform Pressure To Power™, I've been inspired by these techniques as well as my background in sports psychology and human sciences. My main aim with this method is to enable riders to use pressure to perform at their best.

THE PRESSURE PROBLEM

Pressure is a much misunderstood concept. Many riders believe that in order to produce their best performances consistently at competitions, they need to eliminate stress and pressure. This just isn't true. First of all, pressure is a source of energy and you cannot destroy energy. You can only transform it into something else. Second, pressure is a natural feature of competition environments; you cannot escape it. Third, everyone needs a degree of pressure to perform at their best. If you were totally relaxed when you rode at competition, you'd find it difficult to focus, engage your muscles and ride your horse to the best of your capability.

So it's not about escaping pressure; it's about learning how to use it and turn it into something that gives you performance power! That's what this book is all about.

Most of the competition riders I work with are event riders because eventing requires riders to have an extremely strong mindset to successfully complete all 3 phases. I can only work with a relatively small number of event riders because there are only so many hours in the week. But I believe that everyone should have access to these mindset strategies, whether you're just starting out in eventing, whether you're looking to compete at international event level or whether your aim is to ride for Team GB! That's why I've written this book and why I'm giving away 4 free gifts with the book to help you raise your performance level at competitions and ultimately achieve better results.

Here are just some of the things that this book will help you deal with whether you compete in 1 day or 3 day events:

- Stress, tension and nerves before and during competition phases
- If you struggle to maintain focus at competitions
- If you find it difficult to produce the performance level you want at competitions
- Inconsistent performance
- If you want to step up to the next level of competition but are finding it difficult to do so
- Overcoming setbacks

HOW TO GET THE MOST FROM THIS BOOK

To get the most out of this book and start solving these performance problems, it is essential you take action! If you are not ready to do that yet, please put this book away until you are. I really do mean that. I only work with riders who are ready and 100% committed to take action to make changes to their mindset. When they do that, they get great results from working with me. Coaching is a two-way process. To be effective, it requires both the coach and the rider to work together. Think of this book like a coaching session with me. To benefit from it you really do need to take action.

To make it easy, I've highlighted the actions you need to take in each chapter, and here's the first one!

ACTION

Before you continue reading this book, go to my website, www.TransformPressureToPower.com and enter your details to access the 4 free gifts that accompany this book. One of these gifts is a mindset strategy questionnaire that will help you identify the most important areas of your mindset that you need to work on and it will guide you to the chapters that will be most helpful to you. Complete this questionnaire now before you move on to the next chapter.

You, of course, have the option of reading this book cover-to-cover and if you prefer to do that then that's OK. But I know that many of you will be incredibly busy with work and riding so, if you want to start applying these mindset strategies as soon as possible, you'll find the questionnaire a really helpful tool that will give you insight and direction.

Here are just some of the benefits competition riders I've coached have gained from applying these mindset strategies:

- Improved competition performances and results
- Better consistency of performance
- Greater confidence, self-belief and resilience
- Make more quick, accurate decisions
- Deal with challenges at competitions more effectively
- Move up to the next level of competition and perform well
- Overcome setbacks more quickly
- Transfer performance level at home to competition
- Improve skills and performance level more quickly through performance profiling
- Close gap between one level of competition and the next
- Measure, review and apply learning points more quickly

So remember, take the actions I've outlined in this book and apply the mindset strategies consistently and you will improve your performance. It takes 30 days to form a new habit and to do that you need to practise it every day. The more committed you are to applying these strategies the more improvements you will see in your riding, your performance and your competition results.

UNLOCKING YOUR PERFORMANCE POTENTIAL

I believe that every event rider has the ability to achieve their performance and competition goals. Most of the time, I find that it's the rider's beliefs and mindset that holds them back. When I work with riders, I focus on identifying the quickest, most effective route to overcoming these barriers so that the rider can start to unlock their true performance potential. Once this process starts, you gain momentum and confidence which propels you forward and gives you greater motivation and determination to continue.

This book has been designed to help you start your journey of unlocking your performance potential. Before you move on to the next chapter, it's important to check you're in the right place to start this journey.

First, you need to understand that 80% of your success in eventing is mindset and 20% is skill. I'm not just quoting random figures here; this is something that has been extensively researched across many sports through sports psychology and NLP studies. Just imagine for a moment you're watching 2 riders jump a showjumping round. You've been told that they have the exact same level of experience as riders but that one of them lacks confidence and self-belief. How easily would you be able to tell the 2 riders apart? The answer is, of course, that you would find it very easy to tell the 2 apart because the less confident rider would be more likely to make an error in jumping and have one or more poles down.

Second, unlocking your own performance potential can be difficult because of the intrinsic challenges of eventing. Eventing requires you and your horse to be both physically and mentally prepared to take on the challenge of performing well across all 3 phases. Here are the key ingredients required to unlock your performance potential:

- Mental toughness – your ability to overcome setbacks and adversity is critical to your success as an event rider. So if something in one phase hasn't gone well, it's really important to be able to put that to one side and prepare yourself for the next phase. Being able to deal with the highs and lows of eventing is one of the keys to unlocking your performance potential. The path to success is filled with obstacles so the fact that you encounter setbacks means you're on the right track!

- Focus - you need to be able to concentrate over a long period and make quick decisions at speed. There are so many external variables when you're at an event, it's easy to get overwhelmed or focus on the things you cannot control. When you do this, you'll find it difficult to perform at your best. When you fine-tune your mindset, you'll find it easier to focus on the things you can control, which will enable you to perform at your best.

- Motivation – you must feel motivated and excited about making changes to your mindset to achieve your performance goals. You also need to feel equally motivated and excited about going out competing. If you don't feel motivated, you won't take the action required to improve your mindset and so your performance won't improve. If you've fallen out of love with competing, you need to take some time to reflect on why this is and get reconnected with what you love about riding. Once you're refreshed and re-energised, it's time to get out to an event. You will only perform at your best if you feel motivated to do so. You need to be motivated to make a lasting change to your mindset to achieve lasting improvements to your performance. Initially, it can be hard to make changes to your mindset but when you're motivated you'll be able to push through this initial phase and be able to implement lasting changes to consistently improve your performance.

- The 4 Cs – confidence, commitment, control and challenge. You need each of these elements to be well balanced to develop a strong mindset and improve your mental toughness. Each rider needs a slightly different level of challenge to perform at their best. Fine-tuning of each of these elements is critical throughout a rider's career to make sure they consistently produce great performances.

- Switching off autopilot – to make mindset changes you must be willing to invest energy in switching off autopilot! We operate on autopilot most of the time because we have deeply ingrained habits, some of which prevent us from performing at our best. Our brains are programmed to operate out of habit irrespective of whether our habits are good or bad. Most of the time we're unaware of our habits. But you do have a choice about whether to simply keep doing things on autopilot or whether to break the pattern and build a new, more helpful habit that will raise your performance level. When you start to make changes to your mindset and you start to break one or more habits, it will be difficult initially because you have to re-program your brain. However, the great thing about our brains is that they are extremely flexible and there is overwhelming evidence that we can learn new habits at any stage in our life. This means that once you start to switch off autopilot and apply new mindset strategies consistently, you'll be able to build a brand new habit that will enable you to perform at your best and unlock your full potential.

- Self-belief – this is the foundation upon which your confidence and performance potential is built. Belief shapes achievement and achievement shapes belief! Unless you overcome negative, limiting beliefs, you won't be able to unlock your full performance potential. I've dedicated a full chapter in this book to belief, because it's so fundamental to your ability to perform and achieve the results you want in eventing. Once you build greater self-belief, your perspective on your performance will change for the better and you'll gain the momentum and confidence you need to consistently perform at your best.

- Performance zone – to consistently perform at your absolute best, you need to be in your performance zone when you're competing. You're in your performance zone when you're psyched up, motivated, calm, focused and able to make quick decisions. When you're in your zone, you're completely immersed in the present moment, everything flows and you're able to zero in on the task in hand. You may not be aware of it, but when you perform at your absolute best, you are in your performance zone.

These critical success factors are discussed in more detail within each chapter of this book and each mindset strategy will help you unlock your performance potential. Ultimately, it's about taking more control over your mindset. When you do this, you'll be more able to control your performance, and this will improve your competition results.

ACTION

Reflect on your current performance level at competition and identify your top 3 habits that stop you performing at your best. Review your past competition experiences to identify where these habits have come from. Then consider the 3 new habits you'd like to establish instead that would help you to perform at your best. Keep it simple because it's simple changes that are the key to building new habits for peak performance. Keep a note of these habits as you work through each chapter because the mindset strategies you need to start making the changes you want are right here in this book!

DECIDE HOW PRESSURE AFFECTS YOUR PERFORMANCE

Pressure is a natural feature of the competition environment because it's all about putting your skills to the test. In sports psychology, competitions are referred to as "open environments" because your performance and skills are scrutinised by both judges and spectators. This naturally increases the level of pressure that you feel in such an environment. There's nothing you can do to avoid feeling this increased pressure but you can control how it affects you.

Early on in his career, Daniel Scott used to put himself under a lot of pressure to perform, which created tension and nerves. Now an experienced international event rider, Daniel has learnt how to use the pressure of competitions to sharpen his focus and perform at his best.

So it's OK to feel pressure; it's what you do with it that counts!

Many riders find that pressure creates such stress that they are unable to perform at their best. Instead of thriving they struggle. Most of the time, riders do not notice the build up of pressure until it's too late. Whilst pressure is an inevitable feature of the competition environment, there are ways to manage pressure and use it to thrive and unleash your performance power.

When you use pressure to boost your motivation and focus so you get into your performance zone and show what you're truly capable of in the conditions you're presented with at an event, you'll instantly increase your performance power. When you allow the pressure to stress you out and make you anxious, you'll underperform and in that anxious state you'll be unable to unlock your performance potential.

Elspeth Jamieson, international event rider and BE Scotland U18 team member, who was also long listed for the British Junior European Eventing Championship team in 2015, consistently uses the pressure of competitions to focus on how she will ride positively because she has seen the negative effect that a defensive mindset has on performance. She is able to thrive under pressure because she consistently focuses on riding positively throughout her training sessions so that she is mentally prepared when she goes to competitions and able to use her positive, every day mindset to perform at her best.

When you take control of your thinking and actions like Elspeth, you'll have greater influence over your results. When I work with event riders, I focus on helping them identify and make changes to their thinking and actions so they use the pressure of the competition environment to boost their performance. When they do that, the rosettes and placings very often follow.

FROM ZERO TO HERO

There is a massive difference in the mindset and competition outcomes of an event rider who uses pressure to boost their performance power compared with an event rider who allows it to destroy their performance. However, it only takes a small number of mindset changes applied consistently to make this leap from disempowered to super-charged!

All event riders need to experience some pressure to be able to perform at their best. It's just that many riders allow this pressure to build up and it ends up increasing beyond the point that they can manage and when this happens, you get overwhelmed and stress shuts down your ability to perform well.

To transform pressure to power, you first need to make a decision that you're going to take control of how pressure affects you. Studies in psychology show that 90% of what happens is life is as a result of our reactions to situations and only 10% is just what happens. I bet as you read that you were surprised by that! It just goes to show that the reality is you have a lot more control over how pressure affects you and how you perform at events than you thought. That means when you make a mistake or something goes wrong, in 90% of cases, you can fix it and overcome it to improve your performance at your next event.

STAY PRESENT

You can only control what happens now, in this moment. You cannot control what happened a few seconds ago, a minute ago, a week ago, a year ago. You also cannot control what will happen in the future. But by focusing your attention on controlling what happens in the present moment, you will be more able to influence your future outcomes.

WORRYING IS POINTLESS

Getting anxious truly is a waste of your energy. I'm not pointing this out so you beat yourself up about it, I'm simply pointing out that you have a choice about where you invest your energy. It takes just as much energy to worry as it does to focus positively and get into your performance zone. So make a choice to invest energy in being positive rather than fixating on your concerns and worries. Worrying about how you'll perform won't make you perform better because all you'll do is switch on the part of your brain that makes you very anxious and, once you get into that state, you'll find it very difficult to calm down. That's when event riders begin to feel overwhelmed.

ACTION

Examine what specifically you worry about at a competition; for example, is it the spectators, other riders, marquees, the warm-up ring, the process of getting from the lorry to the warm-up, getting round the XC clear? Whatever it is, get really clear on what triggers your worrying thoughts. Then ask yourself what the reasons are for worrying and determine if the reason is a genuine safety concern or if it is simply unimportant to your performance and outside your control (e.g. worrying about what other people are thinking about you). If it is a genuine safety concern, you need to come up with an action plan to deal with that. There's no point worrying about something to do with your personal safety when you can easily take action to deal with it. If it's unimportant and outside your control, you need to change your thinking habits to reduce your stress level and enable you to maintain positive focus.

Make a choice to focus your energy positively. If you're struggling to work out how to do this because you've got a lot of unhelpful beliefs or habits, you'll find the chapters on beliefs, self-talk and focus particularly helpful.

CHANGE YOUR THINKING

You'll already know that your actions determine your results because you'll see this cause and effect relationship happening all the time when you go out competing. You'll probably also know that to get different results you need to change what you do because your riding instructor/trainer will have given you lots of different things to do to improve your horse's focus and way of going. What you might not know is that your thinking determines your actions. Our brains are wired so that we behave in a way that is consistent with our beliefs, values and thinking.

So unless you're prepared to change your thinking, your actions won't fundamentally change, which means you won't achieve significantly different competition results. One rider I worked with was so committed to changing her thinking that she literally went from having multiple XC stops to consistently going clear inside the time within 1 month. Whilst every single chapter in this book has invaluable tools and techniques, it's up to you to apply them consistently to get maximum value from this book.

This book will show you how to set very clear goals that are directly related to your ability to control your performance and influence your horse in the competition environment. My experience with working with event riders is that, when event riders do this focus on their own performance rather than how their competitors are doing or the results of the competition, what actually happens is they perform at their best and very often get the tangible results that they were looking for in the first place.

HOME FROM HOME

Many riders who struggle to deal with the pressure of the competition environment are often frustrated because they know they are capable of performing at a higher level. This doesn't come from being overconfident or arrogant; it comes from experiencing a drop in their performance level at competitions compared with their performance level at home. Some riders report that their riding becomes awkward and clumsy at competitions whereas everything flows much better and feels easier at home. This is because the pressure of the competition environment gets the better of them.

When you are able to use the pressure at competitions to boost your performance you'll perform at least as well as you do at home, if not even better!

The mindset strategies in this book will enable you to reduce this performance differential between home and competition and improve your competition performance so that you are more able to transfer that level of skill that you see and feel at home to the competition environment.

MANAGE IT EARLY

When pressure builds to unmanageable and overwhelming levels, it is often because event riders have failed to recognise the early signs that their stress levels are increasing above a level that is useful. Whilst you need to experience some pressure to get into your performance zone so you can use all your skills to perform at your best, when the level of pressure moves beyond this optimal level, it starts to have a detrimental effect on your performance.

Many riders are unaware of their optimal pressure level and as a result they are also unaware of when pressure starts to get too much. They are unable to identify the early warning signs, which means they are unable to manage their stress levels effectively. Most of the time they don't realise that pressure has built to an overwhelming level until it's too late. By the time they notice it, they're at the competition and their stress level is way above what they need to perform at their best.

As I've already outlined, pressure can either have a positive or negative effect on your performance. The key to managing the effects of pressure on your performance so that you benefit from it is to know the level of pressure you need to perform at your best and then watch out for early warning signs that pressure is beginning to increase above the optimal level for you.

If you and I were working together, we would identify this together and deal with it as early as possible – ideally at least 2 weeks before the competition – to set you up for success. So if you're reading this and about to go to a competition within the next few days, please wait until you're back from the competition before completing the following action. This action requires analytical thinking and if you do it too close to a competition, you may start to over-analyse your stress levels and that won't help you. So please make sure you do this exercise at least 2 weeks before a competition.

ACTION

Think about a time when you performed really well at an event or even in a specific phase (if you struggle to produce a consistently good performance level across all 3 phases). On a scale of 1-10, how much stress were you experiencing? 1 = totally chilled out and relaxed, 10 = stressed to the max. Whatever your score is, this is your optimal level of stress. Everyone's level of optimal stress is different so there are no right or wrong answers here!

Now consider a time when you've not performed well at an event, where you've made mistakes or things have just not gone to plan. Score your stress level again.

Finally think about when you're schooling or jumping at home or at a clinic. Score your stress level using the same scale of 1-10.

Now look at each of your scores and really focus on what you need to see, hear and feel in order to experience your optimal level of stress.

Although I don't know your specific scores, I'd happily predict that your stress level is higher when you've not performed well than when you've performed well, and that your stress level at home is either the same or slightly lower than when you've performed well at a competition.

KNOW YOUR SIGNS

A key part of managing the early warning signs is to know what they are. If you don't know this, it's just guesswork, and every part of your mental preparation for competitions should be precise and focused.

The early warning signs vary from rider to rider so it's important to complete the following exercise to identify the signs that are most relevant to you. As with the last exercise, please only complete this if you are 1 week or more away from a competition. Doing this exercise too close to a competition may cause you to overthink and overanalyse.

ACTION

Review the list of these early warning signs and identify the ones that you experience the most. It will help you to think about your last competition and particularly focus on the last couple of days before the event. Feel free to write in this book – just tick the signs that you feel are most relevant to you. Then once you've done this, review the Mindset Strategy Checklist (one of the 4 free bonuses which accompanies this book – just go to www.TransformPressureToPower.com if you've not already done so to register and access your 4 free gifts) to work out which strategies you'll use before your next competition to deal with these signs. Then work through the related chapter. To help you, I've noted the most relevant mindset strategy against each early warning sign (see page 20). This short exercise has been designed to complement the more detailed questionnaire, one of your 4 free gifts, which I directed you to complete in the previous chapter.

Remember that worrying about things that you cannot control prevents you from performing at your best because you spend too much time, energy and focus on the things that are outside your control rather than on the things that are within your control. For many riders, worrying and getting increasingly stressed before a competition has simply become a habit. So it's important to recognise this and break through the habit to form a new, more positive habit by first becoming aware of what your habits are in the days leading up to an event.

When you recognise and deal with these early warning signs, you'll be able to improve your performance at the competition because you'll be performing closer to your optimal stress level rather than at a much higher and uncontrollable level.

It's important to remember to apply these strategies before you get to the competition itself so that you are able to use the increased pressure at an event to perform at your best rather than allow it to overwhelm you. By managing your stress level before you arrive at the competition, you will be more able to do this. One of the 4 free bonuses you get by registering at www.TransformPressureToPower.com is a cheatsheet that will help you implement all 8 mindset strategies in this book before, during and after each event you attend to enable you to really implement these at the right time.

Warning Sign	Mindset Strategy/Strategies
High and/or unreasonable expectations of myself or my horse	Performance Profiling Beliefs Inner Critic
Unable to eat and/or sleep in the days before an event	Mental Rehearsal Master Emotions
Feeling sick and/or dizzy when I think about the upcoming competition	Mental Rehearsal Master Emotions
Feeling anxious and worrying about all the things that could go wrong	Mental Rehearsal Laser Focus
Become irritable with myself and/or people around me	Beliefs Inner Critic Master Emotions
Start to doubt or question myself	Beliefs Inner Critic
Start to feel intimidated about the size of the event and/or the other competitors	Master Emotions Laser Focus
Become fixated or concerned about the competition result	Performance Profiling Master Emotions Laser Focus
It feels like the upcoming event is a 'win or lose' situation - it really matters	Master Emotions Laser Focus
Feeling unprepared or unorganised	Performance Profiling Laser Focus Rituals & Routines
Worrying about what ground conditions/weather will be like or what questions the XC/ show jumping course will ask	Master Emotions Laser Focus

YOUR PERFORMANCE ZONE

When you experience the right level of stress and pressure, you're able to transform that into performance power because you'll be able to get into your performance zone. The performance zone is a theme throughout all eight mindset strategies in this book because each of the mindset strategies is about helping you to get into your performance zone and stay there!

When you're in your performance zone, you're completely immersed in the present moment and everything flows. You're psyched up and motivated, completely focused on the task in hand. You can make time slow down so that you can make decisions more quickly; you can be entirely focused on the task in hand and be in moment to moment riding stride to stride, totally focused and not distracted by anything else going on around you. When you are in your performance zone you are also incredibly attentive to your horse. You'll know when the horse is asking a question or beginning to hesitate well before a stop or run-out because you'll feel the horse hesitating a few strides back from the fence.

It is the performance zone that enables the world's top event riders to perform at their best and it's what so many of us admire about them; their ability to make adjustments and change their strategy when things aren't going so well. It's because of their laser focus that they will seemingly just be looking into the distance and not paying attention to any of the spectators or distractions around the course or arena.

This book is all about enabling you to tap into the optimal level of pressure you need to perform at your best, and helping you turn that into power by enabling you to get into your performance zone exactly when you need it. If you get distracted you will find and learn new strategies for getting back into your performance zone as soon as possible. This book will also show you strategies for intercepting the early warning signs of pressure, dealing with it and then being able to move on.

My Transform Pressure To Power™ method, which is explained in this book through the 8 mindset strategies, will enable you to take back control of the level of pressure you experience and use that to transform your performance and ultimately improve your competition outcomes and results.

BRAIN POWER

To unlock the power of your mindset you first need to understand how your brain processes information. The human mind has two main processing tools – the conscious mind and the subconscious mind. Each plays an important role in how you learn and recall skills. Both have different capabilities and it's important to understand these to get more insight into how your mind works before you start working on making changes to your mindset.

Back when you first learnt to ride, your conscious mind would have been responsible for learning the skills required so you could sit in the saddle correctly, trot, canter, gallop and jump. To begin with, you would have had to think a lot about your aids, your position and the horse's movement (e.g. forwardness, straightness, etc.). This would have felt tough and you would have made a lot of mistakes. Our conscious mind can only really focus effectively on one thing at a time and when we learn new skills required for riding, we're often trying to learn lots of different things at one. The process can be slow and feel very awkward. Whilst the conscious mind is a very useful tool for helping us to learn, it is a very slow, clunky mechanism in comparison to the subconscious mind, which stores and accesses skills quickly once we have learned and practised them. That is why it is helpful, when learning something new and complex, to focus on mastering one aspect at a time. By breaking down complex learning challenges into manageable chunks, you'll be able to learn more quickly because the quality of your focus will be better than if you try to learn everything at once.

Each time you master something new it is transferred to your subconscious mind where it can be accessed very quickly. Your subconscious mind enables you to multi-task because it requires very little effort to access the skills stored in your subconscious mind. That is why practise is so important because the more you practise a skill the more able you are to access it quickly with very little mental effort.

You will find the example performance profile, one of the free bonuses that comes with this book, a very useful tool that will help you to identify the key skills you need to improve and refine in your practise and it will also help you to break learning challenges down into manageable chunks. If you have not already registered for the 4 free bonuses, then just go to www.TransformPressureToPower.com and enter your details.

PERFORMANCE PROFILING
TO OPTIMISE YOUR RESULTS

The process of transforming pressure into power starts with reducing uncertainty to improve your confidence and belief in your skills, capability and performance level. Performance profiling is a key tool developed by sports psychologists that has been tried and tested across many sports at all levels, from amateur to professional and world champions. The reason performance profiling is so widely used is because it enables you to get clarity on the key areas of your performance and skills where a small improvement will make a big difference to your performance and results.

It enables you to measure precisely your current performance and skill level, then compare it against the level of performance required to achieve your objectives. For example, your goal may be to go double clear and inside the time cross-country at 2 star level, or it may be to qualify for your first international event. Where there are gaps between your current level of performance and the required level of performance, the profiling process allows you to clearly see the size of each performance gap and where the key priority areas are where you need to raise your game. This enables you to start thinking about actions you need to take to close the gap.

PRECISION PERFORMANCE

If you don't profile your performance currently, you may find it difficult to pinpoint the exact areas where you need to improve. Often riders struggle and simply hope that, if they do a bit more practise in between events, they'll be able to make the improvements they want. But unless you're precise in your approach to how you practise and what you practise, you'll find it difficult to make precise improvements in your performance.

When you complete the performance profiling process, you'll be able to identify and address gaps in your current performance level. It's an objective measure of performance and will enable you to identify the specific skills and techniques you need to improve on to achieve the performance level you desire.

Performance profiling works by assessing your current performance level and comparing that against the level of performance you need to achieve your goals. It's useful to think of a rider you admire who is currently achieving the level of performance you want when considering the level of performance you need. In this chapter, I'm going to explain the process and, to give you extra help in completing a profile, I've designed a free gift to help you. It's an example performance profile and to access it, you just need to go to www.TransformPressureToPower.com and enter your details. If you've not already done this, do it now!

Performance profiling is a key performance enhancement tool that enables you to take back control of your performance, and if you have ambitions to move up the levels and even become a successful professional rider (and perhaps a world champion), it is essential that you start using performance profiling.

Whether you're looking to step up to the next level of competition or looking to improve your performance at the current level, performance profiling will help you to analyse specifically what you need to do, what you need to improve and how to improve it in order to raise your performance level.

Performance profiling helps event riders look at the root causes of mistakes and performance issues and analyse how they can improve their performance the next time. How often do you find yourself or other riders blaming a mistake or a performance issue on external factors that they cannot control? Doing this won't help you improve your performance because when you blame something that you cannot control you become less responsible for your performance and less empowered to take control of your performance. It means that, when you compete, you don't focus on the things that you can control that make the most difference to your performance.

So stop blaming mistakes and performance issues on external factors and accept responsibility for taking actions to improve your performance. Know that you have the power to control your performance. When you acknowledge that you have more control over your performance you begin to get more motivated to do something about it, so it's important to take this first step now. Acknowledge that you have control of your performance, and think about all of the things when you go to an event that you can control and influence across all 3 phases.

Whilst the free example performance profile will give you a template, it's important you understand the process of performance profiling, so I'm going to walk you through this step-by-step. When I work with riders, I take them through this quickly because I know how to navigate the process. This means that by working with riders individually I can accelerate the process to quickly identify the priorities and the key actions required to improve performance. Because you'll be completing this process for the first time when you read through this chapter and access your free example performance profile, it's OK if it takes you some time to complete your first profile. The more you use this process, the more familiar you'll become with it, and the more quickly you'll be able to complete it.

ACTION

Complete all the steps in this chapter to complete your performance profile. Make sure you do this when you have at least 2 weeks before your next competition. If you're a few days away from a competition or if you're competing in back-to-back events, wait until you have more time to complete this process. Performance profiling is particularly helpful for planning your practise over the winter break.

STEP 1: GET CLEAR ON YOUR GOALS

To get the most out of performance profiling it is really important that you get clear on what your goals are and what you feel most motivated to achieve, because without motivation and clear goals it is extremely difficult to identify and take forward the improvements so you continually learn and grow your skills to perform at your very best.

We only perform at our very best when we are motivated to do so; this is especially true in eventing. Eventing is a sport known for its highs and lows, and your ability to be mentally resilient and able to deal with setbacks is absolutely critical. Part of the reason that some riders are better at this than others is the level of motivation they have. If you are highly motivated to achieve the results and the targets that you have set for yourself in eventing, the likelihood is you will find a way to do that, and you will be prepared to try and do things that other people are not prepared to do.

Write down all the things you feel really excited and motivated about achieving in eventing. Visualise what you will see, hear and feel once you've achieved these things. Check that your vision of you achieving your goals makes you feel excited, motivated and psyched up.

Once you're clear on what you are motivated to achieve in eventing, it's time to create your goals. When you write your goals, make sure they are:

Specific – be very clear about what you want to achieve

Challenging – make your goals stretching so you have something to aim for as this will build your confidence as you improve your skills and performance

Controllable – focus on your performance outcomes like jumping a clear round, rather than on competition results. Whilst it's great to have an ambition to win, it's more important to have performance goals because these are the goals that you have greater control over and can measure.

Attainable – your goals should be something you can aim to achieve within the next 3, 6 or 12 months. Working towards longer-term goals makes it more difficult to work out the precise steps you need to take to improve your performance. Goal setting and performance profiling should be something you do on a regular basis – at least twice a season – so once you've achieved your goals and improved your performance, you simply define your next set of goals and assess your improved level of performance against those new goals.

Measurable – you must be able to measure how you're doing so you know how much progress you're making and you also know when you've achieved your goals.

Personal – your goals must reflect what you want and your personal ambitions. If you work towards a goal because someone else has told you that you should, you won't have the motivation and determination needed to achieve it. Make sure that the goal is truly something you want.

As you progress and achieve your goals, you'll be able to take confidence from your successes to build and further improve your performance. It becomes a virtuous circle of success so make sure you have clearly defined your goals before you move on. I recommend you create and work towards 1 to 3 goals at a time.

STEP 2: COMPLETE YOUR PERFORMANCE PROFILE

Here's what you need to know to complete your performance profile; and remember to use the free example performance profile you will have received when you registered for the 4 free bonuses on my website www.Transform PressureToPower.com.

It is important that you complete this process as soon as possible after a competition and ideally 2 weeks before your next event. If you are competing in back-to-back events, leave this until you have time to dedicate to completing your profile.

The first part of the performance profile is the performance criteria. These are the measures that you will use to assess your performance. These criteria need to measure the factors that contribute to your ability to perform at competitions. If you look at the example performance profile you'll see a number of different criteria that I use with riders to assess their performance. Here are a few examples of some of the performance criteria I use to help riders assess their performance:

Ability to keep rhythm
Seeing distances
Working the horse in an outline
Balance
Coordination

Staying calm under pressure
Handling setbacks well
Maintaining a positive outlook
Getting on with things following a mistake

The second part of the performance profile is the Importance Score. This means that you need to score how important each of the performance criteria are in enabling you to achieve your goals. That's why it's absolutely essential that you define your goals first before completing a performance profile, so if you've not completed the action outlined earlier in this chapter, do it now! To score importance, use a scale of 1 to 10 where 1 is not important at all and 10 is critical.

Once you've gone through the performance criteria and given a score out of 10 for each one, you're ready to move on and assess your current performance. When you do this, you need to be calm and ready to review your performance rationally and objectively. Only complete this assessment when you are able to do this and can dedicate time to really think about your current performance. If you're stressed out or have other priorities that are distracting you, wait until you are calm and thinking clearly before completing this step.

If you're ready to complete this step, all you need to do is take each criteria in turn and score your current performance level on a scale of 1 to 10 where 1 is poor, 5 is average and 10 is excellent. Think about how well you can perform each criterion right now because that will indicate your level of skill and will help you to determine an appropriate score. At this stage you're just focusing on your current performance and skill level. When you're thinking about your current performance it's vital that you score yourself out of 10 based on the performance you produce at competitions, because this is where you'll be able to identify the key priority areas that you need to improve in order to improve your competition performance and results. The comparison between your current performance and the required level of performance will come later, so just focus on how skilled and competent you are right now.

Once you have assessed your current performance level and scored yourself out of 10 for each criterion, the next step is to score each criterion based on how well you need to perform it to achieve your goals. This is the Required Score. To assess this, you will need to consider the level of skill you need to achieve your goals; you may wish to think about a rider you admire who is currently achieving the results you want at the competition level you are targeting (your current level or the next level up). If you find this step tricky you will find it helpful to ask your instructor or coach for some guidance. Remember they won't be familiar with this process but they may be able to advise you on the level of performance you need to achieve your goals.

When I work with riders I spend time helping them to complete this part of the performance profile because it's a critical part of the process to get right to get clear useful outputs. When you get clear outputs it makes a massive difference to how quickly you will be able to improve your performance and results at competitions.

Sometimes riders are frustrated when they look at the scores on the performance profile because they know it does not reflect the true skill level they are able to produce at home. In this situation, working with a performance coach like myself makes a big difference because you're able to work through these issues in a very focused and targeted way, away from your horse, so that you are more able to produce your best performance at competition.

STEP 3: IDENTIFY YOUR PRIORITIES

It is absolutely vital that, once you have your performance profile, you look through it and look at the scores. You need to identify the areas for improvement, so once you've honestly scored yourself you need to look at the priority areas for improvement.

To do this, make the following calculation:

Required Score – Current Score = Performance Gap
Performance Gap x Importance Score = Priority Score

This makes the process of identifying your key priorities much simpler; just rank each of the criteria in order, starting with the criterion that has the highest priority score.

Next, look at the top 3 priority areas and identify the actions you need to take to improve your performance in these 3 areas. If you identify lots of actions, just focus on the first step you need to take to make an improvement in your performance and to develop your skills further. Write down the actions you will take and by when, and put this document somewhere where you can remind yourself each day of the commitments you've made to improve your performance level.

When I work with riders I focus on helping them to identify both the key priorities and also the quick wins from their completed performance profile. When event riders are able to achieve quick wins and boost their performance quickly, they gain confidence and build momentum to make further changes to further improve their performance and results.

STEP 4: PRECISION PRACTISE

To get the maximum value from this process, it is absolutely essential that you implement the actions you've identified from your top 3 priorities and implement these actions accurately and consistently. When you're refining and learning new skills you must dedicate yourself to practising regularly and consistently. Practise makes permanent!

Olivia Wilmot, international event rider and coach, told me that physical and mental preparation is absolutely essential for success in eventing because preparation helps to build confidence and promote relaxation in advance of competitions. She believes that riders should make every training session count and practise until they are really well prepared, so that they can perform at their current level of competition "with their eyes closed" and are already training at the next level.

It's important that when you practise you are purposeful and focused. It's not just about the number of hours of practise, it's the quality. Research shows that to become world class in any sport, you need 10,000 hours of purposeful practise. To be purposeful, practise must be focused on making improvements and not just focusing on the things you find easy. This means you have to be motivated and committed to making changes and improving your skills so you perform. You need to continually focus on what you want, how to get there and believe in yourself.

Precision practise means practising the things that you are finding difficult and the things that you know you need to improve. There is a tendency to just practise the things that are easy. Often the things we find easy are also the things that we enjoy doing, but this kind of practise is almost pointless. Even if you do hours and hours of practise on things that you find it easy, you will never improve.

It is absolutely essential that you focus your practise on the things that are not going so well, that you need to improve on, and then leave a small amount of time in each practise session to just do the stuff that you enjoy because it's important to get a balance of both. Of course, if the thing you need to improve is something that your horse finds equally difficult, it is important that you take this into account when you practise so that you give your horse sufficient breaks and down time to help them process their learning.

Ultimately your success in being able to improve and enhance your performance at competitions comes from your willingness to take you and your horse out of your comfort zone and work on the things that really matter, the things that you need to improve in order to perform to the best of your ability and potential. I'm going to discuss the subject of comfort zones versus learning and fear zones towards the end of this chapter because it's an important topic that is widely misunderstood.

Ideally, your practise should take place in the 2 to 3 weeks before an event. If you have less than 2 weeks between events, make sure that you finish practising at least 4 to 5 days before the competition. Any practise you do after that will be wasted. For the vast majority of riders, last minute practise is unhelpful because if something does not go well it will affect your confidence going into the competition.

STEP 5: SET YOUR EXPECTATIONS

A key part of the performance profiling process is being clear about the expectations you have of yourself. Many riders I work with set such stretching expectations that they set themselves up for disappointment, and when they don't meet those exceptionally high expectations they believe they have failed. When this happens, you lose motivation and it's tempting to give up.

So it's vital to set your expectations at the right level so that you focus on achieving improvements step by step. When you achieve small improvements regularly you'll find you soon build confidence, momentum and even greater motivation to keep striving to achieve your goals. Remember that performance profiling is a powerful tool that enables you to achieve your goals, and in order to achieve your goals you must be motivated and committed. So make sure you set reasonable expectations for your rate of progress and performance improvement.

Daniel Scott, international event rider recommends that riders focus on competing against themselves and aim to improve their personal best at each competition. He believes that it is important to enjoy yourself and use the competition as an opportunity to seek help and advice from more experienced riders.

Make sure that, when you're at a competition or event, you focus on the performance outcome you want to achieve. If you go to a competition or event with expectations of the result you want to achieve - like being placed or winning - and then find the conditions are not optimal for you or the horse, you'll suddenly feel a lot more pressure. When you get fixated on competition results, you become less focused on all the different elements that make up a winning performance and you can become overwhelmed by the number of things that need to go right in order for you to win. You lose sight of everything you can control at competitions.

So make sure your expectations set you up for success and enable you to continually grow and improve your competition performance.

STEP 6: REVIEW & ADJUST

Once you have set clear and realistic expectations for your performance level and rate of progress, you need to measure your performance so you can track and celebrate progress. It is best to focus on reviewing your performance after you have completed the competition. Doing it at an event will only distract you and take your focus away from the present moment and into the past and future. It's critical that you remain in the present moment at a competition, so wait until you have returned home before measuring your performance.

Remember that the best analysis is done when you are calm and rational, so make sure you get yourself in the right state of mind and are ready and prepared to review your performance.

First, review what went well and make a list. You will find it useful to refer to the performance criteria in your performance profile and score yourself against each criterion based on how well you thought you performed at the event.

Then focus in on what you need to improve and work out how to improve it. If things didn't go to plan at the competition, if you made a mistake or if the horse just didn't perform as you expected, it's vital to focus on what you've learnt to improve your performance next time. To help you focus on the key learning points, here are the questions you need to ask yourself:

- What specifically did not go to plan?
- How did it happen? What happened in the moments before the problem occurred?
- What were your immediate thoughts? How did they influence you? What happened next?

- What are the positives you can take away from this experience?
- What have you learned from this experience?
- What will you do differently next time? What do you need to practise between now and your next competition to prevent this problem?

These are the questions I use when I work with riders who have had a setback to help them bounce back more quickly and focus on what they need to do to improve their performance.

What you learn from any situation depends on your interpretation, and there are multiple interpretations of the same situation. If you find yourself interpreting a situation really negatively, ask yourself "What else could this situation mean?" Find something, anything that's positive. It's important that you take a balanced view of every situation. There are both positives and negatives you can take from any situation.

How you interpret your performance at competitions is critical because it determines whether you learn from the experience and use this to improve your performance. When I interviewed Camilla Kruger, an experienced event rider who was part of the 2015 Zimbabwe Nations Cup Team, she emphasised the importance of learning from mistakes. When things go wrong, she sees it as something that teaches her rather than something that holds her back.

When you consistently focus on asking yourself these questions and answering them, you'll focus more on how to improve rather than beating yourself up. Remember that beating yourself up and being disappointed and frustrated will not help you move forward. It will simply keep you stuck in the past, replaying the mistake or problem over and over again. You need to break free from this to take control of fixing it!

Once you've done this, make a list of the key improvements you need to make and the actions you will take. Then compare these against the actions you've already identified as priorities in your performance profile to check how they align and link in with your key priorities. It could be that something you didn't think was important or a priority when you originally completed the performance profile is now a higher priority and more important.

Next look at the action plan you identified in step 3 and tick off the actions you've now completed that have enabled you to improve your performance. Now look at any additional important actions you've identified from your competition performance and work out how to incorporate these into your action plan. Be very careful to avoid giving yourself too many improvement actions because you'll push yourself too far out of your comfort zone and you'll also make it more difficult for your brain to learn. Remember that your conscious mind, which is the part of your brain that helps you to learn, works best when you only focus on one thing at a time. So remember to keep it simple and focus on the most important things, one at a time!

Remember that winning performances are created through continuous self improvement and focused practise. Your hard work and dedication to continuous learning is what enables you to build your skills and improve your performance, which ultimately enables you to achieve the results you want.

STEP 8: PLAN FOR YOUR NEXT COMPETITION

Confidence and composure at competitions comes from doing the right practise and being prepared.

Remember that you need to be taking small steps forward all the time to improve and achieve your goals. Make sure you set achievable goals for yourself and create a plan of what you need to improve to achieve them. Then track your performance against your plan.

Plan your next competition as much as possible in advance to reduce uncertainty. It's important to have a plan that covers as a minimum the activities you need to complete in the week before, as well as at the event. Having a plan is particularly helpful if you're stepping up from the 1 day event format to a 3 day event.

This plan isn't just about preparing the logistics and equipment, and I know you may be very experienced in this; it's about how you will mentally prepare for getting into your performance zone and staying there in each of the 3 competition phases.

Olivia Wilmot, international event rider and coach, consistently makes a plan for the breaks in between phases so that she can switch off and restore her energy for the next phase. She also structures her plan to allow time to do visualisation and watch specific riders at the event as this helps her to get focused on what she needs to do and how she will ride.

Focus your preparation at home on getting ready for the conditions you will likely experience at the competition, and the outcome you want to achieve. Repeatedly practise until you feel very confident and you are able to complete the course or test with ease and produce the performance you desire.

When you create your plan, think about the unexpected things that have happened at previous competitions you've been to, and consider how you could plan for it and deal with it to gain as much control as possible. When you plan for the unexpected, it will give you a back-up plan that you can use on the day if you need to, and this will give you confidence.

When it comes to the logistics and equipment part of competition preparation, some of the riders I work with prefer to do things last minute. The problem with this is you end up rushing around, your adrenaline and stress level rises, and this means that by the time you arrive at the competition, your stress levels are already above the optimal level for peak performance.

Make sure you have everything you need for the competition prepared in advance so that you can pack up and travel to the competition in plenty of time, feeling calm and in control. This will set you up for success when you arrive at the competition because you'll be more able to deal with any small unexpected things that occur.

Once you've created a competition plan, stick to it! Make sure that the people around you who are supporting you know that you have a plan, and that you need to stick to it. Use the plan to focus on what matters to avoid getting distracted. Take your plan with you to the competition by documenting it on your phone or ideally on a piece of paper to help you remember what you need to do and when.

LOVE YOUR LEARNING ZONE

The phrase "being outside your comfort zone" is one that is widely misunderstood, and all too often riders don't understand the difference between the zones that sit outside your comfort zone – your learning zone and your fear zone.

Whilst you will probably know that being inside your comfort zone feels easy and nice and comfortable, and you can pretty much operate on autopilot and things just happen, you are probably less aware of how far you need to be outside your comfort zone in order to learn and improve. The short answer is you don't need to actually be that far outside your comfort zone. You just need to be far enough out to feel uncomfortable!

So if you are in a situation where you feel challenged and stretched but still able to make decisions and adjust your riding if things don't quite go to plan, you are in your learning zone. You may make mistakes and it may feel awkward at times, but you can adjust your riding accordingly and learn from it.

If you're in a situation where you feel scared and your confidence is low, you've gone too far outside your comfort zone. What's happened is you've gone past your learning zone and into your fear zone. Some of the riders I work with push themselves across into the fear zone in the belief that this is how they will be able to learn and improve more quickly. Whilst it's important to set yourself stretching challenges, when you're in your fear zone your brain is literally unable to learn because when we become scared or anxious, the part of our brain that activates our fight/flight response takes control over what we do and the part of our brain responsible for rational thinking and learning shuts down and is unable to function properly.

Ironically many riders acknowledge the importance of this in training their horses and yet do not realise that the same holds true for humans. A horse cannot learn if it is scared or too far out of its comfort zone, and so most riders approach training their horses in a way that is sympathetic to that to ensure that they learn and they embed new skills. It's important that you apply the same logic and understanding to yourself to set yourself up for success.

Purposeful practise will feel uncomfortable at times but that's a sign that you're making progress. When you find something easy you are operating within your comfort zone. Whilst this creates a nice comfortable feeling, continually operating in your comfort zone does not enable you to grow and improve your skills and performance. You need to be operating in your learning zone to grow and improve. Everyone's zone is different so just work out what pace of learning will work for you. Remember you need to feel uncomfortable and you need to be prepared to work hard. That's what being in your learning zone is all about. You also need to be able to think and work through any problems and when you're in your learning zone you'll be able to do that. If you end up in your fear zone, you'll lose that ability to focus on learning and improving your skills. Everyone needs a different pace of learning so just work out the pace you need to progress at to learn and improve.

When I interviewed Daniel Scott, he emphasised the importance of practise and pushing yourself to be in your learning zone as much as possible to build confidence and self belief so that you are able to perform at your best at competitions.

Remember that every improvement you make is a success so celebrate it!

Being aware of where you need to improve, and specifically the areas you need to improve on, is incredibly important. I cannot emphasise enough how important it is, so you should be feeling good about knowing precisely what it is that you need to improve because it gives you a clear roadmap for how you will improve your performance, your horse's performance and ultimately achieve the results and the level of success that you really want.

HOW BELIEFS UNLOCK YOUR PERFORMANCE POTENTIAL

Do you believe with absolute certainty that you've got what it takes to achieve your goals? It's one thing having goals, it's quite another to believe in your ability to achieve them. Having a strong belief in your skill and ability to perform at your best when you are at a competition, no matter what the conditions, is essential to enabling you to produce your best performances.

Self-belief and self-confidence are inextricably linked. You cannot have one without the other. Once you build self-belief, you gain greater confidence and this grows your self-belief, and so the virtuous circle continues building more and more belief in your skill and ability as a rider.

Many riders associate self-belief and confidence with over-confidence and even arrogance. So when they perform well at a competition, they credit the horse and take very little credit. Whilst world class riders will often do this publicly when they win an event, they will nearly always acknowledge and celebrate their success in private. They know very well the part they played in producing the winning performance and have built such self-belief and confidence in their ability that it does not impact them psychologically when they graciously and modestly accept their win in public. If you do not yet have this level of self-belief and confidence, it is important that you take time to celebrate every success, no matter how small, because then you will build your confidence. The performance profiling strategy I shared in the previous chapter will help you identify and celebrate every small success.

It is important that we deal with the myth that self-belief and confidence result in arrogance. Arrogance can only occur when someone's assessment of their own ability far outweighs their actual ability, and they become complacent about their performance because they have overvalued and overrated their skills. People who indulge in arrogance see no reason to continually learn and improve because in their mind they are already more than good enough! In the case of every single rider I have worked with to date, it is far more common that they significantly undervalue and underrate their ability and skill level. In every case, they have achieved far more than they will ever be prepared to acknowledge, and it makes them feel uncomfortable to acknowledge the true extent of their skill and ability. This means that they lack belief and confidence, and because they have often been underestimating their skill and ability for a while, they find it difficult to break free from it. Much of the work I do with event riders is on changing their perception and beliefs about their skills and abilities. The secret to self-belief and confidence (without arrogance) really is as simple as acknowledging and valuing the skills and abilities you have and challenging any negative beliefs you have about yourself.

So in this chapter, we're going to examine the process of belief change to help you overcome negative beliefs and build greater confidence.

PERSONAL POWER

When you believe something with absolute certainty, it becomes a self-fulfilling prophecy. These self-fulfilling prophecies either empower you to take action and remain resilient when things get tough, or their disempower you, stripping you of motivation, persistence and control over your performance.

Positive, empowering beliefs give you a greater level of control in situations and enable you to take control of your focus and emotions at events so you can perform at your best. These beliefs also support you in learning and improving because you will be more open to constructive feedback and able to learn important lessons when things do not go to plan at a competition.

Negative, disempowering beliefs take away your personal power and although they may stay hidden beneath the surface of your conscious mind most of the time, when your performance is tested at a competition, they surface and start causing chaos, raising your stress levels and making you feel overwhelmed. They are also responsible for making you doubt yourself and for fixing your focus on things you cannot control at competitions, which means that you feel less in control of your performance and you are more likely to make mistakes.

When I work with riders, I often review their beliefs because often it is only possible to fix a mindset issue by going back to the root cause of the problem: their negative beliefs about themselves as a rider. In fact, most of the mindset strategies in this book are most effective and powerful when they are supported by a solid foundation of strong positive beliefs. The bottom line is that without self-belief, your confidence will be fragile, which means you can only maintain confidence when you are in situations where you feel comfortable, and as soon as you are stretched or are required to perform in conditions where you do not feel comfortable, your confidence drops and with it goes your performance. When you have strong positive beliefs, you will be more able to maintain your confidence and perform at your best.

MIND MECHANICS

First it's important that you get familiar with the mechanics of how your mind uses your beliefs so you can understand how to challenge them.

The reason beliefs play such an important role in your ability to perform to your full potential at competitions is because of how our brain processes information. It is a mechanical process that starts with our subconscious mind, which processes every single last piece of data that we see, hear and feel. Right now, and in every second after that, your subconscious mind is processing thousands of pieces of data, from your heartbeat to the weather outside. As you've already discovered in this book, your conscious mind has a very limited capacity compared with your subconscious mind. Whereas your subconscious mind has an almost unlimited capacity for processing data, your conscious mind can only really focus on one or two things at a time. Whilst some people try to divide their attention between multiple things, when they do this, the quality of their focus and thinking rapidly decreases because their conscious mind cannot cope. In other words, your subconscious mind is the master of multi-tasking, unlike your conscious mind. This is why some people get confused about multi-tasking. Multi-tasking only really happens where you are using skills stored subconsciously, alongside your conscious focus on something. Like when you're riding and you instinctively know when to adjust your position before, during and after a jump. This is because you've practised this so much, it's become embedded in your subconscious and now it takes no effort to execute. This means you can focus your conscious attention on something else.

So how does information flow through your subconscious mind to your conscious mind? Well first of all, your subconscious mind needs some rules in order to process and sort through all the data it is processing so it can identify the items that are most important and bring those to your attention. Your beliefs are part of that rulebook that your subconscious mind uses to filter everything you see, hear and feel. This means that your beliefs determine how you interpret situations, what you learn, how you feel about yourself and ultimately how you perform under pressure.

Because everyone's beliefs are different, their brains are operating different filtering systems, and that means that everyone's perception and interpretation of reality is also different. When you change your beliefs, you change your reality! Some riders find this a bit mind-blowing, and really it is, because when you realise that you can take greater control over your reality by changing your beliefs, you open up a whole new world of opportunity to unlock your performance potential.

CHANGING YOUR BELIEFS

So how do you go about changing beliefs? The first step is to challenge them with evidence that contradicts the belief. To show you how to do this, I'm going to give you an example of the common belief about the role of natural talent in determining rider success and then I'm going to give you a summary of evidence that will help change your belief about natural talent.

The belief

I find that many of the competition riders I work with believe that, unless they have natural talent, they won't ever make it as a professional or even world class rider. When you believe this, you will be less motivated and determined to reach your goal. Every time you encounter a setback, you will interpret it as a sign of failure, and confirmation of your belief that you do not have natural talent. This is the way our beliefs work. The more we believe something, the more our subconscious presents us with evidence that our belief is correct, even if there is evidence to the contrary, and this further reinforces the belief. Your brain doesn't distinguish between empowering and disempowering beliefs; it just reinforces the beliefs you hold.

The challenge

This is one of the beliefs that I am very well positioned to challenge, having studied with world class geneticists during my degree at Oxford University. The reality is that human genetics remains a bit of a mystery. Even now, we still don't fully understand all of the genetic code which every human has, and the area where we have the least understanding is how our genes influence and determine our behaviour. Even when scientists think they have discovered a gene that determines behaviour or success in a particular area of life like business or sport, it is so difficult to prove the link in a scientifically rigorous way that, at best, these genetic links are just educated guesses. Most of the time it is incredibly difficult to separate genetic causes from environmental causes.

Secondly, if you think about how quickly athletes can run a mile now compared with 50 years ago, it is crazy. Whereas Roger Bannister's 4 minute mile became famous for being the world record, it has since been broken many times over, and now there are teenagers in secondary and high schools who can run 4 minute miles. This quick progression in our ability to run 1 mile more quickly has not happened as a result of genetics. Believe me, evolution doesn't happen that fast! It has happened because we have developed a better understanding of how to run well, we have better running technology in the form of running shoes, we are able to analyse diet and fitness better and we are more able as a result to design training programmes that focus on the precise skills that athletes need to develop in order to run faster.

Finally, there are examples everywhere of athletes who are not, genetically speaking, well designed for their sports. One example is Usain Bolt whose long legs do not make him ideally designed for running short distances fast. Despite not being ideally designed for his chosen sport, he has adapted his techniques and is extremely successful as a result.

So now you can see how to challenge a negative belief, and if you currently hold a belief about natural talent, I hope that this has started to change your mind and your perspective.

Making the change

Even just accepting this evidence will help you to start breaking this limiting belief down and replace it with a new more empowering belief. Once you've challenged a negative belief you'll be much more able to overcome it and realise that you have a choice in what you believe. In this example, when you choose to believe that professional and world class riders are there because of dedication, hard work and many thousands of hours of purposeful practise (remember it takes 10,000 hours to become world class), your subconscious mind will start to filter based on this belief, and you will suddenly find that you become more inspired and motivated to achieve your goal. You will think of ideas to overcome setbacks and challenges more readily and you will be more determined to succeed, so you will be more able to cope with the highs and lows of eventing.

It is common to find negative beliefs that are out of date. Unless you have consciously examined and challenged your beliefs in the past, it's unlikely that you will have cleared out the old stuff! Because this exercise is not something we are taught to do, our beliefs are not regularly updated throughout our lives, and we can carry beliefs around with us that we have had for a very long time. Riders who struggle with self belief are often working off an old rulebook of beliefs that they've been holding since they were young, and because they have not consciously updated them and challenged them they still hold onto those even though their current reality is actually quite different. This is why beliefs are so powerful. Our reality can change and be completely different but, because we have old beliefs, we still use old filters to interpret and respond to situations.

ACTION

This is a belief brainstorming exercise! Write down everything you believe about yourself and your skills as a rider. Examine each of the beliefs in turn and tick the ones that empower you and enable you to perform at your best, then put a cross against each of the beliefs that have a limiting or negative effect on your mindset, self-confidence and competition performances. Allow yourself 24 hours to complete this exercise because sometimes beliefs that we are not very aware of can surface after your initial brainstorm.

Remember this is an exercise about your perceptions of yourself, and these perceptions and beliefs determine how you interpret situations and particularly how you deal with setbacks. That means there are no right or wrong answers!

Next, work through each of your negative beliefs and identify evidence that contradicts each of these beliefs. To search for this evidence, reflect on your own experience and knowledge, things people have said to you and things you've noticed or observed whilst watching other riders.

Finally, replace the negative beliefs with an alternative, positive belief that will empower you and enable you to perform at your best when you compete. Identify evidence that supports your new positive beliefs. Again, search for evidence wherever you can. It will be there somewhere; it just may be buried because your subconscious mind will not have been filtering for evidence to support the new beliefs. If your new positive belief is something you've not yet been able to demonstrate, that's OK. Just make sure you write it down, in the present tense, and remind yourself of it frequently. So if you lack confidence, you could replace an old belief of "I'm not a very good rider" or "I lack confidence in my ability as a rider" with "I am a very confident rider." You might not feel that yet, but say it to yourself often enough and you'll start to make a shift in your belief and your confidence level.

Remember that, as yet, your new belief is not part of the rulebook that your subconscious mind is using to filter data and present you with your version of reality. This means you are going to need to consciously override the old negative belief and replace it with your new positive belief many times to score it from the rulebook and install the new positive belief instead. Every time you notice an old negative belief, immediately replace it with your new belief. When you do this, you'll start to notice new evidence or you will remember something from your experience that supports your new belief. Write this down and remind yourself of it regularly. If you do this consistently, every day for at least 2 weeks, you will start to notice a difference. Eventually, you won't need to do this anymore because you will have been able to overwrite the old negative belief and your brain will have accepted the new positive belief. You need to do this consistently though, and practise it in order to build your new belief and make it stick!

As you progress with your eventing career, it is very important that you continue to review and challenge your beliefs because as you move up the levels you will need to change your beliefs to keep up with your changing reality.

TURN IT UP!

Negative beliefs can easily overpower your positive, empowering beliefs and this is why they have the power to control your performance at competitions because, when you are under pressure, these negative beliefs rise to the surface and override any positive, empowering beliefs you have.

That's why it is vital to power up your positive beliefs by giving them more attention and focus than your negative beliefs.

ACTION

Revisit your list of beliefs and this time focus on your list of positive, empowering beliefs. Transfer this list to a place where you can easily see and review it every day. You can use a notebook, poster or phone. Write down your beliefs and remind yourself of the evidence that backs them up. Then, twice a day every day for 2 weeks, read them aloud, ideally while looking in the mirror. This is the best way to strengthen positive beliefs. If you feel uncomfortable about doing that, you can just read them to yourself without reading them aloud. Reading them frequently is essential. It will only take you a few minutes every day, so just work out when you will do it and then just do it!

MENTAL REHEARSAL
FOR PRECISION PERFORMANCE

You may not be aware of it, but mental rehearsal is something you probably do on a regular basis. It's just that you probably are not consciously using it to improve performance. In fact, most of the time, we use mental rehearsal to get worried and stressed out! So in this chapter I'm going to explain what mental rehearsal is and how you can use it to improve your performance. When you use mental rehearsal correctly, you'll be able to use it to create better performances and achieve better competition results.

When I interviewed Olivia Wilmot, international event rider and coach, she said that she consistently uses mental rehearsal at competitions to help her get in her zone. For the dressage, she visualises riding through the test and feeling how it will feel. For the jumping phases, she mentally rehearses the courses after she has walked them so she becomes more aware of the course and the lines between fences. This sharpens her focus and helps her to concentrate throughout each phase of the competition.

This is just one illustration of how effective mental rehearsal can help you prepare for the challenges you face at competitions. It is a skill that everyone can develop and in this chapter I will be sharing my top tips to help you improve and develop greater positive mental rehearsal power.

HEADING FOR A FALL

Many event riders use mental rehearsal to focus on all the things that could go wrong and that will hold them back from achieving the performance level and result they want. They play a series of images or a movie over and over in their mind before they go to the competition, which not only increases their stress levels, but also sends a message to their brain that this set of images or movie is what they want! The human brain is extremely susceptible to being influenced by images, so the more you imagine something, the more your brain attempts to recreate those images and movies in real life.

You should think about your brain being like Google. Just like Google, the human brain functions best when you give it precise, specific instructions and keywords. It then goes on a search to locate the information you have requested. The more specific and precise the instruction, the more quickly it produces the answers you are looking for.

Your brain also does not distinguish between real and imagined experience, so whether you are imagining something going wrong at a competition or actually in that situation for real, your brain will treat both as if they are real!

This means that when you practise negative mental rehearsal and you run worst case scenarios through your mind, you not only create vivid images and movies, you also create the thoughts and feelings that go with that scenario so you become tense and anxious. So although you are only using your imagination to think about a situation, you become so immersed that you respond as if you are in that situation right now!

That is why negative mental rehearsal has such a devastating effect on your performance, because if you imagine your horse stopping at a fence or spooking at something enough times, you are instructing your brain to create that situation. Also, when you mentally rehearse in this way, you are building an association between being in a particular situation (e.g. just before a particular jump), thinking stressful thoughts and feeling stressed. This means that when you go into that situation for real, your brain will recognise the situation as one that requires you to feel stressed and will automatically trigger a rise in your stress levels. So what you feared would happen, does happen! This reinforces your negative mental rehearsal and makes the images even more vivid, which means that the cycle of negative mental rehearsal continues.

Some riders find it difficult to break free from this cycle because negative mental rehearsal becomes a habit and therefore they are often not aware that they are stuck in this cycle. However, being aware that this is happening is the first and most important step to breaking the habit.

REHEARSAL IS PRACTISE

Mental rehearsal is also a form of practise that compliments your ridden practise. Because your brain does not differentiate between real and imagined experience, you can continue practising even once you've untacked your horse, and refine your skills remotely!

When you practise negative mental rehearsal, your practise is focused on not using your skills effectively and not riding to the best of your ability.

For mental rehearsal to be effective as practise, it is vital that it is very specific and clear. It must be tailored to you, the level you are currently competing at and your key areas for improvement. When I devise a mental rehearsal plan and scenarios for riders, I often just work on one specific skill or aspect of their riding performance at a time. Once they have mentally rehearsed it and refined that particular skill, we move on and work on something else.

RELEASING THE HANDBRAKE

Negative mental rehearsal prevents you from performing at your best. You need to think of it like a handbrake because it blocks your performance. It does not allow you to take calculated risks or make quick decisions. It slows you down and holds you back!

When you make a shift from negative mental rehearsal to positive mental rehearsal, you release the handbrake on your performance and even just one small change in your mental rehearsal habits can make a big difference. Positive mental rehearsal has the power to build your confidence, motivation and resilience. It helps you master your emotions, maintain positive focus and gets you ready for being in your performance zone throughout all 3 phases. It's a fantastic strategy and that is why I wanted to share it with you in this book because it really does help you improve your mindset and performance in a number of different ways.

So if you struggle to maintain your concentration and your focus and stay in your performance zone, positive mental rehearsal will really help you improve in these areas. It will also improve your confidence in situations where you are experiencing something for the first time, e.g. your first international event, because you will be able to convince your brain that you have already performed in those conditions in advance of the competition. We always feel less confident when we are facing a situation for the first time and after that initial test, we start to feel increasingly comfortable. Positive mental rehearsal can help deal with those 'first time' moments and create a more positive experience.

Just as negative mental rehearsal can produce the very scenario you were dreading, positive mental rehearsal can produce the exact performance outcome you want! In the same way that negative mental rehearsal is reinforced by the same negative experiences, creating a vicious circle, positive mental rehearsal allows you to create a virtuous circle. This means when you vividly imagine performing something well at a competition, your brain then makes this a reality at your next competition and so you feel more confident, which reinforces the images and movies in your mind and means you continue to practise this positive mental rehearsal.

Here are the main benefits of using positive mental rehearsal to improve your performance level and consistency:

- Improves your skills
- Enables you to plan ahead to deal with a particular challenge
- Allows you to take greater control over your emotions
- Builds your confidence

By using positive mental rehearsal, you will gain a greater sense of control at competitions, which enables you to deal with any challenges you face throughout the 3 phases. Then you will truly have performance power!

TOP TIPS

Here are my top tips to get the best from positive mental rehearsal:

- Engage all your senses in creating a series of images or a movie so you really experience the scenario you are rehearsing.
- Make the images or movie very clear and bright.
- You need to see yourself in the pictures or movie riding your horse and you need to clearly see exactly what you are doing.
- Just rehearse one thing at a time.
- Make sure you're relaxed when you practise. A relaxed mind is a receptive mind!
- Practise it frequently to embed the positive experience, learning and improve your performance. The more familiar you are with the scenario and what you are doing in it the more able you will be to recreate that experience at a competition.
- The most common mental rehearsal scenario I get riders to work on is visualising how they will ride their test or course accurately at their upcoming competition because this helps you to remain calm and focused in the competition environment.

ACTION

Make a list of all of the scenarios your regularly think about, either through imagining a picture, movie or through story-telling (i.e. an internal narrative). Now review each one and tick it if it has a positive effect on your performance and a cross if it has a negative effect.

Now review the list of negative mental rehearsal scenarios and work out which one has occurred most often at a competition. This is your priority scenario to focus on and, at this stage, you need to put the other negative mental rehearsal scenarios to one side and return to them after you have successfully dealt with the priority scenario.

Next, work out what alternative scenario you could rehearse that would enable you to produce a positive outcome. Now create a series of images or a movie in your mind of this new positive scenario. Make sure you see yourself and your horse in these images/movie and make it big and bright. See how you are riding, what you are doing and how your horse is responding. For example, if you imagine riding towards a cross-country fence and your horse stops, imagine instead that you are riding positively before the fence and getting the right rhythm, then see yourself and your horse clearing the fence.

Focus on practising one thing at a time and keep it really simple. This is about creating new positive outcomes, and that can only happen when you are calm and focused.

If possible, create this scenario in your ridden practise at home before the competition so that your positive mental rehearsal and your practical ridden practise are aligned. This will allow you to continually reinforce the positive scenario using real and imagined experience.

I recommend that you mentally rehearse your new positive scenario 3 times every day. By doing this regularly you will be more able to turn your imagined experience into reality at competitions.

Remember that to get different results you need to take different actions, so by doing this practise every day, you will be more able to achieve better results.

TRANSFORM YOUR INNER CRITIC INTO YOUR BEST SUPPORTER

Maintaining a positive attitude is absolutely essential to being able to deal with the highs and lows of eventing. If you struggle to maintain a positive attitude, it's useful to understand the source of it, and one of the main ways to do this is to start tuning in to your internal dialogue. We talk to ourselves all the time, whether we are aware of it or not. If your internal dialogue is positive, you will focus on the positives in any given situation. If, however, you indulge in negative thinking, you will not focus on the positives and only see, hear and feel negatives.

When Daniel Scott, international event rider, described how he gets himself prepared and in his performance zone, he mentioned that he always says the same thing to himself so that he gets psyched up and ready to perform at his best.

It's important that you always choose where to place your focus because wherever your focus goes your energy follows. So if you focus on talking to yourself negatively, your attention on what's happening in your external environment also turns towards the negative aspects. What that means in a competition environment is that your focus is likely to shift to the things you cannot control rather than the things you can control. What that also means is you have less control over your performance. So making sure that your inner critic is well under control is a key mindset strategy that will enable you to improve your performance simply by maintaining your focus on the aspects of your performance that you can control at competitions.

STORY-TELLING

Once you tune in to your inner voice and listen to what it is saying, you will notice that your inner voice is in the business of story-telling, In fact, we tell ourselves stories all the time. We commentate on everything from our interpretations of particular situations to how we think we are doing. In telling ourselves these stories, we either support ourselves or we beat ourselves up. Often we talk more harshly to ourselves than we would ever dare with other people but sometimes this leaks out, and for some of the riders I work with, their inner voice occasionally leaks out and they start snapping at the people who are at the competition to help and support them.

The type of story we tell ourselves often depends on the situation we find ourselves in. For most riders, their inner voice tends to be positive when they are not in a pressurised situation (i.e. riding at home) and becomes negative when they are under pressure or feeling stressed.

Just like when we read a story in a book or see a story being played out on screen, our internal story-telling can evoke powerful emotions, particularly when we are already feeling stressed. This means your inner voice is able to trigger positive or negative emotions depending on the story you are telling yourself. When it is positive, it has the power to make you feel confident and in control, which allows you to make quick, effective decisions. When it is negative, it can be incredibly destructive. When we talk negatively to ourselves, we are effectively telling ourselves scary stories. Just like a horror film, these stories conjure up scary pictures and feelings that impact on our energy, motivation and confidence. This is particularly damaging when you are competing because it progressively eats away at your performance power over the course of the 3 phases and can ultimately destroy your performance if you do not keep it in check.

Some riders believe that a negative inner voice is necessary for success in eventing because they believe their inner critic keeps them focused on what they need to improve and prevents them from becoming over-confident. However, the reality is that a critical inner voice does far more damage than good. I have worked with riders whose inner critic is so loud and so demeaning that they freeze at competitions, unable to make decisions and perform because their inner voice has raised their stress level to such an extent that they have become completely overwhelmed. In less extreme cases, riders simply doubt themselves and feel anxious, which means that they are more likely to make mistakes during their test or round.

CHOOSE YOUR POSITION

There are 3 positions that your inner voice can take and, throughout every day, the position of your inner voice will normally change and flex between all 3 positions.

- **The Dreamer** – this is also known as wishful or aspirational thinking. It is healthy to indulge in this from time to time because this is where your imagination can really be let loose and you can come up with new ideas and solutions to help you overcome problems, identify new goals you want to work towards and reflect on new ways to improve your performance.

- **The Realist** – this is the voice of reason. It is not overly critical or positive; it takes a balanced view of the world. When you have a foundation of strong, positive beliefs, this voice will be encouraging, balanced and instructive. It is your best supporter and the voice you need to perform at your best at competitions.

- **The Critic** – this voice judges everything negatively. It looks for flaws and then magnifies them. It is quick to generalise, so if for example, you misjudge a stride going into a fence, your inner critic might say "I'm so stupid, I always get it wrong." It is more than likely that you are not in fact stupid and that most of the time you get your strides right, but the inner critic ignores that fact. The inner critic asks a lot of negative why questions like "Why can't I get this right?" and "Why does this always happen to me?" The inner critic thrives on stress and nerves, so to get it to shut up, you must first examine your beliefs and then manage your stress level so it does not rise above the optimal level for performance, so you can keep it under control.

TUNE IN

To deal with your inner critic you first need to tune in and notice what you are telling yourself, and the specific words being said. It's also useful to work out if there are key phrases that are regularly repeated. If a pattern of recurring phrases emerges, that normally means that this negative self-talk is being driven by one of your beliefs, and to overcome it you need to work out what the belief is and challenge that. Where there is a pattern, you must go back to the source of the problem to get a long-term fix, because if you do anything else it will just be temporary. You need to reprogram your mind!

Some riders find that there are no recurring patterns but that their inner critic is active most of the time, even when they are relaxed. This means that they have got into a habit of speaking to themselves negatively. Often this comes back to their level of self-confidence, so it's helpful to look at your beliefs if you think your inner critic is active most of the time. There are also a variety of tools and techniques I use when I work with riders and it depends on their specific situation as to which ones work best. The important thing to remember with a dominant inner critic is that you can control it. Most of the time, riders with a dominant inner critic are speaking to themselves in this way out of habit. Over time, this habit has been reinforced because the focus of the rider has been on the negative aspects of multiple situations, which has allowed the inner critic to continually criticise and blame the rider for those negative things.

The most significant and detrimental effect that an inner critic has on your ability to perform at your best at a competition is that it tells your brain to do the exact opposite of what you actually want. If you hear your inner critic saying things like "I really hope I don't mess this up" or "Don't make a mistake with the striding to the next fence," you are giving an instruction to your brain to do the very thing you do not want! Sometimes riders use these negative commands when describing their performance plan for the next phase with other people, so listen for this and if you notice negative commands, you need to turn them into positives. So in the example of "I really hope I don't mess this up" you could replace it with "I am going to ride this positively and calmly."

The other problem with a dominant inner voice is that riders pay far too much attention to it at competitions, and this takes their energy and attention away from their horse and their riding. This energy and attention, which should be directed towards the challenge at hand, whether it be dressage showjumping or cross country, is focused inwardly to something that adds no value. This means you are much more likely to make a mistake. When this happens, the inner critic becomes even louder and even more unpleasant, which means you are likely to make more mistakes, and so the vicious circle continues.

The only position that is useful to you when you are competing is the realist voice, because this is the voice that is your best supporter and is also able to provide positive, specific instructions on what to do next so you can ride stride by stride, moment to moment. This means that you are more able to focus on what you can control in the moment; you are more positively focused and therefore more able to make quick decisions. When you quieten your inner critic and invest your energy on focusing on the things that really matter, you will be much more able to build your confidence and deliver the performance you want.

When you allow your inner voice to take the realist position and move that voice so that it is at the front and centre of your mind, you will suddenly find that your critic has been transformed into your best supporter.

I once participated in an experiment at a training course where I was blindfolded and asked to throw a ball towards a target on the floor. Obviously because I couldn't see the target I would not know whether I had hit it or whether I was even close. The other attendees had been instructed to give me negative feedback initially, so when I threw the ball for the first few times, they said things like "You're miles away," "That's no good," "You call that a throw?" – you get the idea! It meant that every time they gave me this feedback I felt a lot less motivated to continue participating in the experiment , which meant I gave up trying to perform at my best and meant my performance got worse rather than improving. When they switched and started giving me positive feedback like "You're close, keep going" and "You're doing really well," I tried harder and each time my performance improved so I got a lot closer to hitting the target.

So what happens when you allow your realist voice to become more dominant (and you shut your inner critic up) is you encourage yourself, which means you work harder, you gain motivation and you're much more likely to be able to deal with challenges and find a way to perform at your best, whatever the conditions or questions being asked at the 1 day or 3 day event.

SWITCH OFF AUTOPILOT

The key to dealing with your inner critic is to practise switching it off before you go to a competition. Remember that as soon as your stress level increases, your inner critic gets stronger and has more power. To help you manage your inner critic you will find the Mindset Cheatsheet, one of the free bonuses included with this book (go to www.Transform PressureToPower.com if you have not already registered), really useful so go get that now if you have not already registered.

You will find it much easier to challenge and deal with your inner critic when you are away from the competition environment and are relatively calm. Remember that to overcome a habit, you have to consciously notice it and override it for a number of times in order to break the habit and make a new, more positive one. So here are 3 simple steps to switching off autopilot and transforming your inner critic into your best supporter:

- **Step 1:** Tune in to your inner critic – notice the words being used and notice how that is making you feel. Notice if the words are following a pattern or continuous loop. Write down the key phrases that are making you feel tense, stressed or worried.

- **Step 2:** Challenge your inner critic – imagine that your biggest fan or your best supporter is with you right now. What would they be saying to the inner critic? How would they be challenging your critic? What exact words would they be using? Write these words and phrases down in a notebook or make a note of them in your phone. These words need to be somewhere that you can easily access when your inner critic starts to take control. Memorise at least one of those positive phrases so that you can use this when you are riding.

- **Step 3:** Interrupt and replace – there are lots of ways to interrupt your inner critic and my favourite ways are to say "stop" (either out loud or in your head), pinch yourself (if you are riding do this on the back of your hand), or take a very long deep breath and notice the cool air going in through your nose and warm air going back out your nose. Once you've interrupted your inner critic, replace the negative noise with your positive supportive phrases that you noted down in step 2.

Remember this is all about regaining balance and perspective.

If you are having a bad day, remember that one bad day is just that and nothing more. Just as you have had great days where everything has gone really well at competitions in the past, you will have those days again. Sometimes bad luck just happens and, when it does, it is tempting to think that you are destined to encounter more bad luck. But the more you take control of your performance, the more good luck will come your way! Be determined to create your own luck, and by taking control of your inner critic you will be much more empowered to do just that!

ACTION

Complete steps 1 to 3 as outlined above. If you believe your inner critic helps you or if you unclear about whether you speak negatively or positively to yourself, ask yourself "How does this help me perform at my best?" When you get clear on specifically how your inner dialogue helps you, the value of your inner voice is clear and, in the situation of the inner critic, you will get much clearer on how exactly this critic is holding you back from performing at your best.

When you are tuning in to your inner critic in step 1, check your energy levels and consider if the energy level you are feeling is sufficient for performance. Remember that your inner critic will lower your energy levels by progressively destroying your motivation and confidence. Think about how your inner critic is affecting your energy levels and score yourself on an energy scale of 1 to 10 where 1 is no energy at all and 10 is fired up and ready to go!

In steps 2 and 3, think about the words and phrases you will use to tap into your best supporter and bring your realist voice to the front and centre of your mind. Think about how this affects your energy levels and score yourself again on a scale of 1 to 10 where 1 is no energy at all and 10 is fired up and ready to go!

DEALING WITH SETBACKS

Your inner critic loves setbacks! It thrives when you make mistakes, you have a bad day or if things just do not go to plan. It waits until you are at your lowest ebb and then it pounces and attacks you. This means that, when you experience a setback, you need to be alert to the danger of your inner critic resurfacing, particularly if you are in between phases at a competition and something has not gone to plan in your previous phase. Perhaps you feel you were marked harshly for your dressage or you had a stop cross-country, or you had a pole down in the showjumping. Whatever it is, you need to regroup quickly and, to do this, you need your inner voice to take the realist position.

It's OK to have a moment of frustration. What isn't OK is to beat yourself up. When you do this, your inner critic wins and you lose!

To get your inner voice to switch to the realist position, remind yourself of all the things you've done that have made you successful. Think about what you have learnt from experiencing the setback and what you will do differently next time. Doing this automatically turns a negative into a positive.

You need to practise and get good at getting in touch with your inner realist as quickly as possible. To do this, just use the key words and phrases your best supporter would say to you to override your inner critic and refocus on the positive. You can use the same 3 simple steps I outlined earlier in this chapter to help you, and remember my Mindset Cheatsheet will also help so make sure you go to my website and register to receive this and 3 other free gifts if you have not already done so.

It's really important that you develop this skill. I cannot emphasise enough how important it is that you master this mindset skill. If you simply beat yourself up all you're doing is stripping your self-confidence and resilience, and it isn't going to help you perform better (remember the blindfold experiment I mentioned earlier).

CHAMPION YOURSELF

It's part of our culture in the UK that we think it is boastful to celebrate our successes rather than downplaying them. Many of us downplay our successes or we congratulate the fact that the horse made a massive effort in order to detract from our own success. We do this partly because of our mindset but partly because our culture dictates that we should do that.

When you fail to acknowledge these things, your inner critic starts to gain power, so take time out to celebrate your successes and acknowledge what you have achieved. This will boost your confidence and improve your skill in interrupting and overriding your inner critic. In short, it will get you better connected with your best supporter and the realist position that you want your inner voice to take.

Doing this means you will have the energy and focus needed to bounce back quickly from setbacks and focus on all the elements of your performance you can control, so you are more able to produce your best performance and achieve the results you want. It means when the going gets tough, you get going!

MASTER YOUR EMOTIONS

Emotional control is absolutely essential to enable you to perform at your best at competitions. The part of your brain that controls emotions is separate from the intelligent, super-computer part that makes quick, accurate decisions and allows you to apply all of your skills and experience to a situation. The super-computer part of your brain is called the pre-frontal cortex and it is extremely demanding. In order for it to work effectively it needs a lot of energy, and so if the emotional centre in your brain is very active, it consumes so much energy that the pre-frontal cortex cannot work effectively.

Therefore, being able to control your emotions isn't simply a psychological technique, it's a biological and mechanical imperative. The bottom line is that you will not be able to perform well at a competition if you are experiencing highly intense emotions.

For some riders, just knowing this fact is helpful because they get stuck in a vicious cycle of getting very worried and stressed, then beat themselves up for not performing well, which makes them even more stressed. When you understand that to perform better you need to reduce the intensity of the emotion you are feeling and you take action to make this happen, you will instantly improve your performance level.

Just like pressure, emotions are a form of energy and so they are not things you can simply remove from your competition experience. So it's not about eliminating emotions, it's about reducing them and controlling them at a level that enables you to direct your mental energy to your pre-frontal cortex.

This is a skill that successful international event riders have mastered. In fact, when I interviewed Camilla Kruger, it was very clear to me that she has great skill in this area and has used this to help her move up through the levels. By remaining level headed and practical throughout each phase and day of an event, Camilla is able to structure her time in a way that helps her remain focused on the present moment, prevents overthinking and means she can effectively control her heart rate and stress level. This helps her to see the competition as "just another day in the office."

Throughout this chapter, I'm going to be explaining exactly how to master your emotions and, rather than going into a lot of technical detail about the brain, I'm simply going to show you how to gain greater control over your emotions and activate your pre-frontal cortex. This entire chapter is really all about allowing your pre-frontal cortex to work because whilst it is the best piece of technology you own (yes, really), it is extremely demanding and unless it has exactly the right conditions, it will not function properly. Think of your pre-frontal cortex like a diva. You need to meet its demands first before it will perform for you!

NOT ALL EMOTIONS ARE CREATED EQUAL

The world's top riders are able to exert such control over their emotions that they are able to stay in an optimal state that enables them to perform at their very best. They are able to access emotions that empower them whilst minimising the impact of negative emotions like stress, tension and nerves. So whilst it is essential that you feel psyched up, motivated and ready to perform, if this becomes stress, nerves or any other negative emotion, you start to lose control and your emotions start to control you. This means that not all emotions are created equal and you need to be aware that negative emotions will control you whereas positive emotions enable you to take control and get you ready to perform at your best. This is a key part of how event riders can transform pressure into power, by overriding negative emotions and replacing them with positive, empowering ones.

When negative emotions take control and overpower event riders, it is common for riders to experience 'choking.' This is a phenomenon observed in all competitive sports where the competitor becomes so tense and overwhelmed with negative emotion that they start to over-analyse and overthink, which means their energy is being invested in the wrong place and leaves no capacity for them to execute their skills effectively. This means that they underperform even though they are capable of producing a much better performance. This happens to a lot of riders I work with, who become so worried about jumping a clear showjumping round that they overthink the striding and approach to a jump and end up having poles down. So to avoid 'choking' you must learn to master your emotions.

Olivia Wilmot, international event rider and coach, recommends that riders focus on keeping things simple and straightforward to avoid overanalysing their performance. She also recommends that riders break down challenges into manageable bitesize chunks that you can deal with as this will help you to remain focused and gain control over your emotions.

EARLY WARNING SIGNS

The first and most essential step for mastering your emotions is learning how to recognise the early warning signs. In an earlier chapter I outlined the importance of identifying the early warning signs of pressure, and since pressure and emotions are interconnected, it is vital that you intercept negative emotions before they overwhelm you. Pressure and emotions have a driving effect on each other – when one increases so does the other. However, when you are able to take control you can reduce the pressure you experience by reducing the intensity of your emotions.

Becoming skilled at mastering your emotions is all about being able to identify and intercept the early warning signs because this is when the emotions are at a relatively low intensity and it's easier to control them. If you wait until the intensity has built and you feel overwhelmed, you'll find it much more difficult to regain control because you'll have used up a lot of mental energy by that stage.

So here are some of the early warning signs you need to look out for:

- Feeling worried, anxious, tense or stressed
- Headache, loss of appetite, tired or lethargic
- Poor quality and/or quantity of sleep
- Drop in motivation level
- Negative self-talk
- Worrying thoughts
- Feeling compelled to double-check everything
- Visualising worst case or what-if scenarios

These are the most common early warning signs that I come across in my work with competition riders. When you are able to recognise and deal with the early warning signs you will instantly gain more control over your performance.

ACTION

Think about the last time you felt negative emotions overwhelming you at an event and write down the exact emotions you were feeling in that situation. Labelling the emotions helps you identify the source of the problem. For example, nerves are often a sign that you lack confidence or self-belief. Next, think about what was happening before you felt overwhelmed and identify the early warning signs. You can use the signs I listed earlier in this chapter to help you. Think about what triggers these early warning signs – is it a negative belief, your inner critic or just general worry or concern?

To help you examine the trigger points, I recommend you refer to the mindset strategy cheatsheet which is one of the free bonuses that comes with this book. Just go to www.Transform PressureToPower.com to claim your free gifts.

IDENTIFY, INTERRUPT, REPLACE, REPEAT

Once you've started to identify your early warning signs and have more insight into what triggers negative emotions and when, the next step is to identify it when it happens, interrupt it and replace the emotion with something else.

Remember that emotions are energy and you cannot destroy energy; you can only change it and transform it into something else. This is what this step is all about. You're looking to make a mindset shift from being in a right state to being in the right state!

Interrupting the negative emotion means that you stop it in its tracks and prevent it from escalating and controlling you. It means you take back control and can use your skills and experience to make quick, accurate decisions. It means you can perform to the best of your capability, and when you consistently interrupt and take back control of your emotions, you will find you perform better and more consistently throughout all 3 phases of an event.

Over time, the more you interrupt the negative emotion, the less power it will hold. By consistently interrupting the emotion every time you encounter your trigger and replacing it with a more empowering emotion like confidence, you will break the association between the trigger and feeling the negative emotion like stress or anxiety. At the same time, you'll also build a new association between the trigger and feeling confident. Once this new association is established, you will have achieved a shift in your mindset by creating a new, empowering habit that helps you to perform.

So let's say for instance that you currently feel worried every time you start walking the showjumping course. This is something that happens every time and you may not even be aware of it because it's an automatic response that your brain produces every time you walk a course. Your brain has learnt to associate the course walk with feeling worried and tense. By interrupting this emotion and replacing it with calm confidence every time you walk a showjumping course, over time you will break down this habit of worrying and instead you will simply feel calm and confident when you walk a course.

Interrupting a negative emotion can be as simple as taking a deep breath and just acknowledging what is happening. You may find it useful to say "stop" either in your head or out loud as an interruption strategy.

To replace the negative emotion you are experiencing, you simply need to choose an alternative, positive emotion. It could be confident, happy, excited, motivated, calm, rational. All of these emotions will help you to redirect your mental energy to the part of your brain that needs to work well for you to perform at your best.

Then simply repeat as often as possible to embed a new empowering emotional habit. By practising this process you will not only establish a more useful habit that enables your brain to function well, you will also build your skill in mastering your emotions.

The reason this mindset strategy has such a powerful positive effect is because most of the time, you are unaware of your emotional habits, and so because you are not aware of them, you also do not challenge them. This means that habits that hinder your performance simply get repeated over and over again automatically, and over time this simply serves to reinforce and strengthen the habit. Once you recognise these emotional habits, interrupt them and replace them with a more positive, empowering emotion, then you can start to form a habit that will enable you to perform at your very best. The more you practise, the more able you will be to embed the new empowering emotional habit. I work with some competition riders every week for one month because research shows it takes 30 days of consistent practise to embed a new habit.

Negative emotional habits can also be created by your belief system and your inner critic, so it's important to examine your beliefs and inner critic (refer to the chapters earlier in this book) and challenge those to help you overcome negative emotional habits.

ACTION

Work out which positive emotion you will replace negative emotions with and then commit to implementing the identify-interrupt-replace-repeat process I've described every day for 30 days.

STRESS TEST

Emotional mastery is not just about being able to control your emotions; it's about being able to quickly connect with your optimal emotional state for performance. You may remember I mentioned that the pre-frontal cortex is demanding. Well, it has a very specific set of demands. In order to work at it's very best, it needs energy in the form of blood flow, and lots of it! Unless you are in an optimal emotional and physical state, your pre-frontal cortex will not get enough oxygen, protein and glucose and so it will not be able to function at its best. So you need to be in an optimal emotional state to enable your brain to perform optimally.

When you are in an optimal emotional state, you will be motivated, psyched up and ready to go. You will experience pressure and a level of stress, but you will be using this to get prepared and ready to compete. You will use this stress to get really focused on the task in hand, whether it's dressage, cross country or showjumping. Everyone needs a different level of stress to be in this optimal emotional state and so it is important that you identify the exact level of stress you need to perform at your best.

Your optimal emotional state is what allows you to get focused and into your performance zone. Without your optimal emotional state you will not be able to get into and stay in your zone because the part of your brain that actually enables you to be in your performance zone is, yes you've guessed it, your pre-frontal cortex!

ACTION

Think back to the last time you performed really well at a competition and think about how you felt. What thoughts were going through your mind? What was your focus and concentration like? How would you describe your emotions? Then think back to the moment where you first began to feel like that at the competition, and think about how you were able to get into that optimal emotional state. In between events, practise getting into this optimal emotional state when you are riding so that you are more able to get into this optimal emotional state at events.

EMOTIONAL SCALES

One of the main reasons competition riders decide to have 1-2-1 coaching sessions with me is that they find it difficult to manage their emotional scales. They find that excitement turns into nerves and motivation becomes anxiety. Managing your emotional scales is important because it helps you to also manage your energy levels. I think of emotions as being on a scale where the positive emotion is on the left and requires less mental energy, and on the right you have the negative emotion that requires more energy, like this:

Low energy drain	High energy drain
Motivated	Anxious

Where are you on this scale when you go to an event? Are you closer to the motivated or anxious end? Although everyone needs a different level of motivation to perform at their best, most riders who perform consistently well at events will be somewhere around the motivated end of the scale.

Remember that when you feel intense negative emotions that your pre-frontal cortex, the part of your brain responsible for making decisions and accessing your riding skills cannot work properly, which prevents you from producing the performance you are truly capable of. We have a price to pay for the very sophisticated technology that we have in the pre-frontal cortex and that price is mental energy. Because our pre-frontal cortex burns through energy really quickly (if it was a car it would be a sports car!) you have to be really careful about how you use your mental energy over the 3 phases. This is why mastering your emotions is a really powerful mindset strategy and it is also why, when we feel intense negative emotions, we find it difficult to take back control because … guess what? The part of your brain that helps you take back control of your emotions is your pre-frontal cortex so that is why recognising and interrupting the early warning signs is so important.

That is why understanding where you are on your emotional scale and managing your emotional state is so important, because positive emotions can quickly become negative and overwhelm you when you are under pressure, which means you can quickly lose control of your emotions and your pre-frontal cortex is unable to work properly. When you allow your emotions and the pressure of a competition environment to control you, you lose your ability to think and ride positively. That also means that your horse is likely to become uncertain about what you want and will be more hesitant or distracted.

To really master your emotions, you must be prepared to switch off autopilot mode and complete the exercises I've outlined in this chapter. You need to increase your self-awareness to catch negative emotions early before they become overwhelming. I won't lie, it will be hard work. However, I promise that it will be worth it.

TROUBLESHOOTING

This section outlines a few of the most common problems that competition riders I work with are experiencing, and my suggested solutions:

- **Unable to let go of setbacks**
  Many riders struggle to let go of setbacks they have experienced or mistakes they have made in a particular phase. This means that their mental energy gets drained throughout the rest of the event because they are focusing on the setback or mistake and beating themselves up. If you experience this, you need to interrupt your inner critic as it is usually your inner voice that does the beating up! Remember our inner critic is strongest when we are feeling stressed, tense, nervous, frustrated, angry or disappointed. It thrives on negative emotions. Next, you need to take a step back and think about the most important thing that you need to focus on right now. Every time you start thinking back to the setback or mistake, refocus on what you need to do right now. You can only control what happens in the here and now. By doing that you will be more able to influence the future. You certainly will not be able to change what has happened in the past. Remember that when you believe that failures and errors are a sign that you won't ever succeed, it's inevitable that you'll feel disappointed and frustrated, and you'll feel like giving up. However, it's only when you

give up that you truly fail. Everything else is a source of valuable feedback and learning points. In the moments where you haven't succeeded, ask yourself, "How could I use this to improve my performance next time?" This will focus your attention on what you have learnt, and when you learn, you set yourself up for future success.

• **Feeling emotionally drained and fatigued**
This happens when riders do not conserve their mental energy during an event. Remember that this is an endurance test for your brain and you need to conserve energy in between phases. Use the breaks in between each of the phases to relax. Relaxation does a number of things: it lowers your heart rate, it lowers your blood pressure and it also allows you time to conserve your energy. If you spend the breaks in between each phase worrying about your current placing or worrying about what's coming next, you're wasting precious energy. Remember that the only thing you can control is what's happening in the present moment so just focus on the here and now and take some time, even if it's just a few minutes, to relax. There are a variety of different relaxation techniques you can use. Try relaxing the muscles in your arms in your legs and take a few deep breaths, then relax the muscles in your face and neck. This will bring your focus into the present moment, quieten your mind and help you think about what you need to be doing right now in order to set yourself up for success in the next phase. When you conserve energy in this way you also allow your brain to have more energy to make quick decisions when you need it most. Elspeth Jamieson, international event rider and BE Scotland U18 team member, recommends that riders organise their time to relax and resist the temptation at 3 day events to start thinking about the next day until it's there. She is able to control her focus at events because she organises her time well.

- **Feeling demotivated when things have not gone to plan**
  The best antidote to this is to make sure you celebrate your successes when they happen. No matter how small the success, make sure you take time to acknowledge it to yourself and enjoy the moment! Celebrating successes is really important for motivation. If you don't celebrate your successes, you lose motivation to keep going when the going gets tough. Make sure you acknowledge when things go well and write them down in a journal so you can remind yourself of previous successes when you encounter a setback. Even when you experience a setback, reflect on what went well because something will have gone well; it's just that we lose sight of this when we're disappointed and frustrated. Acknowledge what has gone well so that you gain a more balanced perspective of the situation.

- **Creeping, crippling nerves**
  Many riders I work with don't know they are nervous until they are struck by an attack of nerves at a competition. Experiencing nerves is normal but it's about having control over them that makes a difference between staying calm under pressure and becoming overwhelmed. The solution to this lies in the Identify-Interrupt-Replace-Repeat process I described earlier in this chapter. Follow that process and you will soon find that nerves no longer creep up on you!

- **Fear of failure**
  Even when you have tons of motivation and commitment, fear of failure can really hold you back. Fear of failure really kicks in when you really want to win. Overcoming fear of failure makes all the difference to your ability to unlock your potential and achieve your ultimate eventing goal. To illustrate this, let's imagine we're looking at the mindset of 2 riders, both of whom are highly motivated to produce winning performances.

Rider A has a low fear of failure. This means that Rider A approaches every competition full of energy, even if the conditions are not great and the outcome is very uncertain. Rider A will take calculated risks and will be incredibly determined and resilient to overcome setbacks and keep going to achieve their ultimate goal.

Rider B has a high fear of failure. This means that whilst Rider B takes personal responsibility for their outcomes, mistakes, problems and setbacks cause self-doubt and damage self-confidence. Rider B worries about failing a lot, which means they're less likely to be able to move past setbacks and less persistent in continuing to work towards achieving their ultimate goal. This means that Rider B is very unlikely to fulfil their potential.

Where's your motivation coming from? Is it coming from an internal source – e.g. a sense of achievement or is it coming from an external source – e.g. wanting external recognition, sponsorship, awards, rosettes, titles? Once you understand your motivation, you need to make sure you set performance goals, not outcome goals, so you focus on achieving things that you can control and you have more control over your performance than you probably realise.

DEVELOP LASER FOCUS IN EVERY PHASE

You cannot expect a great performance without focus, and you need to make sure your focus is on the things (technical and/or psychological) that will enhance your performance. When you develop laser focus, you will be able to access your performance zone exactly when you need it in each phase. Laser focus is what helps you stay in your performance zone and protects you against distractions. It's like a protective bubble where the only things you notice are you, your horse and the next movement or jump in the test or course.

Whilst there may still be the rare occasion that you get distracted, because sometimes things just happen (like a loose dog on the cross country course for example), laser focus enables you to refocus and get back into your performance zone within a split second rather than taking several seconds to refocus or maybe not refocusing at all!

Laser focus allows you to make quick decisions and adjustments so that you are more able to deal with whatever happens on course or during your test. You'll have much more clarity of thinking because your mind will be quiet and you'll be able to focus entirely on the task at hand. Laser focus is a fundamental feature of your performance zone.

This is a skill I see in all successful international event riders and for many riders, laser focus is a critical part of their competition strategy. When I interviewed Camilla Kruger, she said that remaining focused in the present and living each moment to the full at competitions is critical for success. Olivia Wilmot, international event rider and coach, also commented on the importance of remaining sharp and focused throughout all 3 phases.

Your focus is like a mental spotlight. Whatever you focus on is what you see and experience, whilst everything else is cast into shadow. When you change your focus, you change what you see, hear and feel. It gives you an entirely new perspective on a situation. That is why your focus is so important when you are at an event. When you consistently achieve the right level of focus in all 3 phases, you will be more able to perform consistently at your best.

KNOW YOUR TARGET

Without motivation and clarity on what you want to achieve, it can be difficult to maintain laser focus. Because it's so energy intense, you have to be really motivated to maintain it so you focus on the task at hand and ignore absolutely everything else. Whether you're riding a dressage test or jumping a course, it has to be the single most important thing to you in that moment. If it's not, your focus is likely to wander.

So, the first key to developing laser focus is to always know what you want to achieve from each event. Remember to focus on the performance level you want to achieve rather than the result because it's during your performance that you can exert the most control. Once you are clear on the performance level you're aiming for and you're feeling motivated, you're in a great place to get focused.

GET THE RIGHT QUALITY

The recent digital age of technology means we are increasingly being asked to divide our attention between 2 or more things. The human brain is pretty useless at dividing attention between multiple things and, whilst technology perhaps makes it a little easier for us to do this, it's not a strategy that works at competitions.

Our conscious mind can only really focus with accuracy and quality on one thing at a time, and when we ask it to do more than this the quality of our focus decreases. When that happens in a competition situation, your conscious mind starts to become overloaded and this is quite often what will trigger stress tension or nerves. You start to worry or doubt yourself or get stressed by the number of things that are going on. Your brain goes into overdrive and this is when you start to overthink, overanalyse and override.

So if you do a lot of multi-tasking, you need to rethink this at competitions. It can be difficult to develop laser focus if you're used to getting distracted regularly on a day-to-day basis when you're at home and not competing. However, when you compete it is absolutely essential that you are 100% focused on the task at hand, whether it's riding your dressage test, negotiating a ditch or a double in the showjumping. When you give something 100% attention to the exclusion of everything else going on around you, you are laser focused! Laser focus is absolutely essential for helping you to stay in your performance zone. Without it, you will find yourself getting distracted very quickly.

In order to win an event many things have to go right. The trouble is if you focus on all of the things that have to go right two things will happen. First you feel overwhelmed by the level of challenge in front of you. It is a bit like wanting to climb Everest and all the way up simply staring at the top. If you did that you would soon lose focus on putting one foot in front of the other and getting to the top. Second, you try to focus on too many things and that is when your brain starts to overanalyse and micromanage absolutely everything, rather than allowing things to flow and just taking one thing at a time. Developing laser focus in each phase is all about your ability to focus on one thing at a time.

So to develop laser focus, you first need to make sure that you are completely immersed in the task at hand, whether it's dressage, cross country or showjumping, because you need to remain in the present moment. Secondly, you need to focus on one thing at a time. It sounds simple, doesn't it? It is; it's just that it's not easy, and that is why it is a skill you need to develop.

CHOOSE YOUR DIRECTION

Laser focus is not just about quality of focus, it's about direction. If you direct your focus on to something you cannot control, you will find it difficult to stay in your performance zone. To stay in your performance zone you need to be focused on what you can control and nothing else. That means distractions, your inner critic, anxious thoughts and thinking about the result or placing you could achieve, all needs to be put to one side. These things lead you down a path of focusing on things you cannot control. In this chapter, I'm going to explain what you can do to improve the direction of your focus so you stay in your performance zone.

Many riders I work with become fixated on their results, particularly if they are going into the final phase with a low penalty score and are within touching distance of winning. This is when their focus is likely to wander and they will not be 100% focused on the task at hand. At no point should you be thinking about your result until you have jumped the final fence of the final phase and crossed the finish line. Up until then, the only thing you should be focused on is the task at hand.

Other riders I have worked with have experienced issues in the showjumping ring because they were getting distracted by things that they knew their horses would not like, such as sheep, umbrellas, flags, marquees. As soon as they focused on these distractions, they became less focused on jumping, and that was when mistakes occurred. Because these distractions could not be eliminated from the competition environment, the riders had to learn to simply ignore them and remain focused on jumping the course, one jump at a time, even if their horse got distracted and they had to refocus the horse. By making this one simple change, their showjumping performances improved significantly.

Whilst it's tempting to time travel to the past or the future when you're competing, it's essential you stay focused on the present moment. When you do this, it means that, if something doesn't go to plan, you just move on and focus on the next thing you have to do to complete your round or test.

Elspeth Jamieson, international event rider and BE Scotland U18 team member says that a key mindset change that made a big difference to her performance at competitions was changing the direction of her focus so that now, she only focuses on the things she can control which calms her mind and enables her to concentrate on performing at her best.

From the moment you enter the warm-up to the moment you complete your round or test, just focus on one step at a time. Forget everything you cannot control, just focus on what you're doing right now and you'll find it easier to make adjustments and quick decisions.

ACTION

Make a list of all the things that tend to distract you at competitions. Then look at each one in turn and work out how you could avoid getting distracted in future. Practise at home if possible and use mental rehearsal (see earlier chapter) to help you with preparing for dealing with the distraction. Often we react to distractions out of habit so you need to take action to break that habit.

PRACTISE PRODUCES FOCUS

Remember that laser focus is a skill that you need to develop and, in order to do this, you must practise.

First, you need to complete the action in this chapter and then practise achieving the right quality and direction of focus at home. It is important to practise laser focus at home because it's only here that you will make improvements. Remember that the competition environment is all about testing what you can already do, so if you haven't improved your focus by the time you get to an event you will not improve it simply by being at the event. So you need to be able to focus consistently well at home before you can expect yourself to be able to produce the same level of focus at competitions.

Because laser focus is more mentally demanding and intense, you will not be able to sustain it for very long. Laser focus is a little bit like a muscle – you need to build strength and endurance over time. First, you need to measure how strong it is now by setting a stopwatch and timing yourself whilst riding at home to see how long you can sustain laser focus. Then practise laser focus at home every time you ride for 2 weeks. Then measure your laser focus again using a stopwatch and see how much improvement you have made. The maximum amount of time you should be aiming for is 20 minutes as it is extremely difficult to sustain laser focus for much longer than this because of how energy intense this mental skill is.

When you are practising this skill, make sure you are breathing. If at any point during your practise you are not breathing deeply enough, there will not be enough flow of oxygen going to your brain to maintain laser focus. I know first-hand about oxygen deprivation from doing high altitude skiing in the USA a few years ago. The village was at 3,000m above sea level and the highest ski run was 4,500m above sea level. For the first few days, I found breathing and walking pretty tough but trying to use my skiing skills was exceptionally tough. I also could not focus on anything for any length of time. I knew how to ski but couldn't seem to make it happen, and because I couldn't focus very well I was very clumsy for a few days until I acclimatised. This was because there was not enough oxygen getting to my brain and so my pre-frontal cortex was not able to work properly so I couldn't access my skiing skills or focus on anything very well. After a few days this effect wore off because I acclimatised but it was a great example of how important oxygen is for mental focus and physical performance.

RITUALS & ROUTINES
TO BOOST YOUR PERFORMANCE

Rituals and routines are key mindset tools that enable you to switch yourself into performance mode and get into your zone. You may have noticed that professional sports people have routines that they always go through before and during competitions. Often these routines are labelled as 'superstitions,' which makes them seem like they are frivolous and irrelevant, but they are actually the key to helping the athlete or sports person unlock their performance potential.

The reason routines are labelled as 'superstitions' is because they have meaning to the competitor using them but they may have no logical or rational meaning to other people. You can argue that triggers, which I cover in the next chapter, fall into the same category. It doesn't matter if the routine, ritual or trigger makes logical sense or not; it just needs to help the competitor perform at their best. If it serves that purpose, that is what matters.

Obviously in equestrian sport, there is the horse to consider in all of this and so any routine, ritual or trigger must be safe for the horse and rider, and it must also not compromise the horse's ability to perform. So for example, a warm-up routine must effectively warm up the horse to prepare it for the athletic challenge ahead and prevent injury, whilst also helping the rider to get focused and in their performance zone.

In this chapter, I'm going to outline some of the most common rituals and routines that help event riders. These are repeatable processes that you can use as often as you need to throughout all 3 phases of an event.

EFFECTIVE ROUTINES & RITUALS

Effective routines and rituals give you certainty, control and a plan of action. When you are at an event, you are competing in an environment that is often uncertain and unpredictable, so having routines and rituals in place will give you reassurance and a greater sense of control.

Routines and rituals are essentially about getting you into your performance zone and helping you to conserve vital mental energy and control your emotions.

Camilla Kruger, international event rider and Zimbabwe Nations Cup Team member, told me that she has a series of routines that she has designed and refined in training at home so that when she goes to competitions, she focuses on doing what she's trained to do at home.

This is a great strategy because it provides Camilla with greater control and an ability to more easily transfer her performance level at home to the competition environment.

Make sure you plan each event knowing which rituals and routines you need in order to be successful, because this will help you focus on yourself and what you need to do to perform at your best. If you are competing in a big class, this will help you to manage the pressure of other riders because you will be more focused on your performance.

Here are the most common rituals and routines that I find are most helpful for event riders:

- **Pre-competition**
  The purpose of this routine is to help you stay organised before competitions and focus your attention on the upcoming event. This type of routine covers everything from the last work session you do with your horse before an event, to the process of packing your lorry or trailer for an event. It is common for riders to have a series of these pre-competition routines that they carry out in the final week before every event. This is a routine that I will explain in further detail later on in this chapter.

- **Warm-up**
  Having a warm-up routine is good for you and it's good for your horse, particularly if you ride young or inexperienced horses. Routine gives horses comfort in the uncertain and unpredictable environment of a competition. It also has the exact same benefit for you and, because it gets you focused on riding each step of the routine, it enables you to get in to your performance zone. The better you know the routine and the more precisely you ride it, the more effective the routine will be in a competition environment. So make sure you practise it at home and know it back to front!

- **Refocusing**
  Have a routine or ritual that allows you to refocus and get back in your zone quickly. This could be a deep breath, saying something to yourself or simply riding a shape like a 10m circle to give you time to refocus. This will help you to limit the impact that distractions have on your performance and help you refocus more quickly.

- **Mental rehearsal**
  As well as being a mindset strategy (see earlier chapter) mental rehearsal is also a routine that you can use to switch yourself into performance mode.

PRE-COMPETITION ROUTINES

The reason I'm dedicating a section of this chapter to the subject of pre-competition routines is that very often a mistake made at an event can be directly linked back to the pre-competition routine and preparation of the horse and rider. Whether you're aware of it or not, you already have pre-competition routines and rituals; it's just that they may be unhelpful rather than being something that aids your performance.

One pre-competition ritual I have come across is something I call 'the wind-up.' Some event riders use the time before an event to get nervous and wound up about the conditions and the challenges they may face. Clearly this isn't going to be helpful to them on the day, as it is merely building up their stress levels in advance of the event, which in itself will raise their stress levels.

So it's important that you establish some clear pre-competition routines as well as event routines and rituals that help you manage your stress, conserve your mental energy and get you ready to switch into performance mode and get into your zone!

Effective pre-competition routines are essential for getting you in the right state of mind to perform at your best and get the competition outcome you really want. These routines will give you a greater sense of control going into the competition and will help your horse remain calm.

The best pre-competition routines are simple. Keeping it simple means your routine will be predictable and easy to repeat for every competition.

This will give you a greater sense of control, and the predictability of the routine will help keep your horse calm. Write down everything you believe you need to do in order to prepare for the competition, including what exercise routine your horse needs to perform at his/her best. Being clear about the optimal plan for your horse is essential. This will depend on your horse's preferences and fitness. Only you will know what works for your horse; just make sure you have a clear plan that gets your horse prepared and ready to perform. Once you've completed your list, go through it and evaluate the importance of each item. Check that you have included the essential things like checking your horse's shoes, packing your equipment, food, first aid kit, etc.

Your pre-competition routine must include a deadline for finishing up practise. This is really important because last minute practise can be damaging to your competition performance, especially if you are struggling with something, like a section of your dressage test. It is much better to practise the things that you are finding difficult and could be the weakest link in your performance way before you get to the competition, because trying to fix that last minute will likely damage your confidence and not set you up for success.

The next element you need in your pre-competition routine is a routine for eating, sleeping and just generally taking care of yourself. To make sure you have sufficient mental energy for all 3 phases of your event, it is very important that you rest and eat well in the week leading up to the event. Your muscles also need to be well rested and this needs to be balanced up with the riding preparation you are doing.

Your pre-competition routine needs to be designed to reduce your stress so that you're not leaving things to the last minute and so that you are well-prepared. This means preparing all the logistics well in time and knowing when you're going to do things like plaiting up and loading equipment on to your lorry.

STRUCTURE IS YOUR FRIEND

Build a checklist for the event itself to help guide you through the event so that if things start to get overwhelming, you can simply review your checklist and identify the exact thing you need to do next. This will help you focus and give you back control. This is where you will find my Mindset Strategy Cheatsheet useful. It is one of 4 free gifts that accompany this book. If you do not already have access to these, simply visit www.TransformPressureToPower.com to get them now!

Be completely open with your support people, or whoever comes with you to competitions, about what you need from them in order to remain calm and focused. Remember rituals and routines are all about giving you control and allowing you to remain calm under pressure, so make sure you're really honest with the people around you about what you need them to do for you so you can implement the rituals and routines you need to get into performance mode and into your zone in each phase.

DESIGN YOUR OWN

So now you know more about the most common routines and rituals that help event riders get switched on and into their performance zone, it's important you understand how to design your own rituals and routines. This is something I help competition riders with so I have a lot of experience and here are my top tips:

- Keep it simple! Simple routines are more powerful than complex ones so make sure you keep it simple.
- Remember the aim of a routine is to help you stay organised and feel in control before and during competitions so you can focus your attention on your performance.
- Focus on creating a routine or ritual that enables you to be in peak state and remember that what works for other people might not work for you – find what works for you and stick with it!
- Make sure your routine or ritual enables you to get into your performance zone, so you quieten your inner critic and maintain the right level of stress and pressure that enables you to thrive and perform at your best

ACTION

Make a list of all the rituals and routines you use before a competition currently and include all the unhelpful ones as well as the ones that help you perform at your best. Then design new routines and rituals using the information and tips in this chapter that you will implement in place of the unhelpful ones so you remain calm, in control and ready to perform at your next event. You will find it useful to refer to my Mindset Strategy Cheatsheet which is one of 4 free gifts that accompany this book. If you do not already have access to these, simply visit www.TransformPressureToPower.com to get them now!

DEVELOP TRIGGERS TO UNLOCK YOUR PERFORMANCE POWER

This final mindset strategy is really powerful once you have established a strong set of positive beliefs, a good level of focus and you have control over your inner critic. For triggers to be effective, you need to have a good level of self-awareness, which each of the other mindset strategies in this book will help you build. It is also useful to have a good awareness of the routines and rituals that work well for you at the moment as that will give you direction and insight to finding triggers.

Triggers are different than routines and rituals because they are much shorter interventions and are designed to instantly switch you on and get you into your performance zone.

Just as triggers can be powerful tools that unlock your performance power, many of the riders I work with also have negative triggers, and if you find that as you work through this chapter you're identifying a number of negative triggers, revisit the chapters on beliefs, mental rehearsal, inner critic and master your emotions. If you've already done this and you're struggling to overcome negative triggers, please email me explaining your situation and the problem you're experiencing and I'll give you some advice and guidance. My email is: Helen@Transform PressureToPower.com

UNDERSTANDING TRIGGERS

Triggers are a natural part of human behaviour, and over your lifetime you will acquire numerous triggers, most of which you will not be consciously aware of. When I talk about triggers in this chapter, I am describing a stimulus-response process; that is, your brain produces a behavioural response to a stimulus. In NLP, we call this 'anchoring' and I often use this with riders to help them develop new triggers. The process of establishing and using triggers has been studied for a long time in psychology and perhaps the most famous of all studies in this area is Pavlov's dogs. In this experiment, the dogs would salivate every time a bowl of food was produced. The researchers then presented the food and at the same time rang a bell. They repeated this process over and over again. Then they rang the bell without the food being presented to the dogs and the dogs salivated. This experiment demonstrated that not only is it possible for the brain to form new associations, but those associations do not necessarily need to make logical sense. For instance, why would it be logical for a dog to salivate just at the sound of a bell? The thing was that the dogs had learnt that the bell and the food had a connection and therefore their brains associated the sound of a bell with food and produced the same behavioural response (salivating) as if they had actually been presented with food.

This is why, when we observe the so called 'superstitions' of world class sports people, we think they make no logical sense but it's very likely that these superstitions are acting as triggers that enable them to get into their performance zone. It makes no logical sense to us because we do not see the association that the sports person is making between the 'superstition' and being in their performance zone. These 'superstitions' are often either triggers (small movement that triggers a response) or a ritual (a series of movements).

So when you read through this chapter, it will be useful for you to understand this background and the fact that every trigger you have has been created by your brain learning to associate a particular stimulus – a sight, sound, movement – with a behavioural response – excitement, nerves, anxiety.

The response part of the trigger can have one of three different effects – positive, negative or neutral. When I work with event riders, I focus on identifying positive and negative responses. I enhance and strengthen the positive responses and help riders use these when they need them the most, and I also help riders to reduce and remove negative triggers. I can usually break negative triggers pretty quickly and riders are often surprised by the speed at which this is achieved. The reason for this is that your brain makes associations between different things all the time and is constantly updating its database of causes and effects. This means that, depending on how deeply embedded the association is, you can break it pretty quickly and replace it with a new one. Neuro-linguistic programming (NLP) provides some great tools and techniques for achieving this, which is why I am a big advocate of using NLP techniques when I work with riders.

ACTION

Think back to the last event you were at and identify when you may have been using triggers. Remember that you may not have been aware of them so just think about any situation where you noticed yourself making a switch or a change between one behaviour and feeling to another. Many event riders I work with have a trigger at the point that they move from the warm-up to the arena or start box. The point at which they move forward into the arena or start box triggers a feeling of nerves or anxiety. This is just one example and it is a negative trigger. You will probably have examples of both positive and negative triggers so just think through what those are and make a list. Then look down your list and highlight the positive ones. Make a new list of the positive ones and keep this with you at events so you can remind yourself of the triggers you can use to help you get into your performance zone. It is important to note here that positive triggers are most effective when you use them occasionally. If you use them too often they start to lose their effect. This means that sometimes you may be able to overcome negative triggers by repeatedly exposing yourself to them until you learn that there is no negative consequence. There's a reason I have used the word 'sometimes.' It is relatively straightforward enough if it's something relatively low risk like public speaking. Let's say that you got nervous every time you stood up in front of a crowded room to speak. Repeatedly exposing yourself to this would, over time, reduce the power of the negative trigger. However, because we are discussing triggers here in the context of equestrian sport and eventing, which is a high risk sport, it's really important that any attempts you make to overcome a negative trigger are done in a very controlled and safe environment because any negative triggers you have when riding may well exist because of a genuine safety concern. That's why I advise you seek help from a qualified professional to overcome a negative trigger, especially if you have completed the actions I gave you in earlier chapters and you're still struggling to deal with a negative trigger.

POSITIVE FOCUS

Before we move on and look at how you can develop your own positive triggers, it is important that you understand the type of responses that you are looking to achieve as a result of the trigger. Most of the triggers I use with the riders I work with 1-2-1 are designed to trigger positive focus. Positive focus is the key that unlocks your performance zone.

Positive focus is basically a combination of laser focus and having a positive mindset, which you will develop through the strategies on beliefs, mental rehearsal, inner critic and emotions. This is why I have deliberately placed this chapter on triggers at the end and why I mentioned at the start of this chapter that, to get the best from triggers, you really need these other mindset strategies in place first. Because once you have these in place, you can work out how to trigger positive focus.

Everyone experiences positive focus differently so it is important that you get connected with what positive focus feels like for you. Here are the most common features of positive focus that many riders experience:

- Motivated
- Psyched up and ready to go
- Focused
- Confident
- Time slows
- In the zone
- Unaffected by distractions
- Quiet mind
- Breathing slowly
- Only aware of yourself, your horse and the next challenge (dressage movement or fence)
- Tuned in to your horse
- Able to make quick decisions and react quickly
- Remain focused in the present moment
- If a mistake occurs, you simply move on and focus on the next movement or jump

GET TRIGGER POWER

1. **Focus on what you want**
   The first step to trigger positive focus is to focus on what you want. For positive triggers to be really effective in a competition situation, it's very important that you do this first. Think about the performance level you want to achieve. Remember that you need to focus on something you want that is within your control. Being placed or winning is not something you can control.

2. **Identify a trigger**
   Triggers are very individual and vary from rider to rider. This step is all about tapping into your own experience rather than trying to copy someone else. What works for them won't necessarily work for you.

   Remember that a trigger is something that produces a behavioural response. It will be something you have learnt, just like Pavlov's dogs. I am a big fan of identifying quick wins, and when it comes to identifying a trigger, your quick wins are hidden in amongst your life experiences.

   When I work with riders I ask them a series of questions to understand what positive triggers they currently have in other areas of their lives outside riding that could be repurposed and used in a competition situation.

   Think about things that make you feel calm, confident, in control and positive. Make a list and identify some triggers. If you're struggling to identify an existing positive trigger from other areas of your life that will give you positive focus, here are some examples of triggers you could use:

- Song – music can often hold powerful triggers. I have a song that I play every time I'm preparing for a workshop because it helps me get into my zone. I don't play it at any other time because I want to maintain its power.

- "Lucky socks" – this can be socks or another piece of clothing that makes you feel good. It doesn't have to make you feel lucky, it can simply make you feel powerful and in control, as if it gives you some magic super power. The important thing here is that it triggers positive focus for you so it doesn't matter if you think it's superstitious. If it has the desired effect, that's all that matters!

- Catchphrase – words have meanings and can evoke powerful emotions. Think about the words and phrases you use when you're in your zone. Perhaps it's something you say to your horse like "Get on" or "Let's do this." The best catchphrases are the ones that are stated positively. Avoid negative phrases like "Don't mess this up." Negative phrases are negative triggers. Whatever the phrase is that works for you and makes you feel switched on and in your zone, you can use it as a trigger by saying it out loud. You can say it as quietly or loudly as you need; just make sure you say it confidently and calmly.

- Focus words – this is similar to a catchphrase except focus words tend to just be single words that give you a command that helps you to get into your zone. For example, if you tend to get tense in the warm-up, you may wish to use "Relax" as your focus word. Remember that, whatever focus word you choose, it must give you the desired response, so in the example I just gave, saying "Relax" will only be a trigger for you if it actually helps you to relax. It's best if you say your focus word out loud and remember you can say it as quietly or loudly as you need; just make sure you say it confidently and calmly.

- Action – sometimes just doing something helps switch you on. This is the type of trigger that most people associate with superstitions. In tennis, you see players bouncing the ball a set number of times before they serve and, each time, they bounce the ball the same number of times. They are using this as a trigger, a cue, to get into their performance zone. As a rider, there are so many actions you have to do before you even get on your horse, that you could use pretty much anything, but remember that it needs to produce the exact response you want. It must help you get into your performance zone. Examples of actions that some riders have used include buttoning up their jacket or zipping up their body protector, zipping up their riding boots and putting spurs on. These triggers act as a signal to get into your performance zone, so think carefully about the actions you take at events currently that help you to get into your zone. Remember that most of the time you are unaware of your triggers and this exercise is all about becoming more aware of what your positive triggers are so you can use them strategically at events.

- Mascot – this is a small object that you carry around with you. This could be absolutely anything but it needs to be small and safe enough for you to have with you in all 3 phases. It needs to be something that you associate with being in control and feeling good. The idea of a mascot is that you can touch it when you need to get into your zone or if you simply need a confidence boost.

- Affirmations – these require practise before the event and are positive phrases designed to make you feel confident. An example would be "I meet every situation knowing I am its master" or "I confidently overcome whatever challenge is in my way." If you say these phrases repeatedly every day you'll start to build strong belief in them, and then you can use this as a trigger to help you feel confident when you need it at events.

To help you identify your triggers, write this sentence down and fill in the blanks for anything you think is a trigger so you can clearly see the cause and the effect and work out if it helps you get into your performance zone:

When I see/hear/feel/experience (BLANK), I feel/do (BLANK)

3. Plan when to use it

Once you have identified your triggers you then need to work out when you will use them at each event. It is best use triggers when you really need them the most. For most event riders, I recommend that they use the triggers during the warm-up because it is critical that you are in your performance zone by the time you go into the arena or start box to start your test or course. If you get nervous before the warm-up, I recommend that you use a trigger when you first get on your horse before you go into the warm-up. This is also a useful strategy if you are about to enter a busy warm-up arena. You can also use a trigger to refocus yourself just before you enter the competition arena or start box. You can also incorporate triggers into your pre-competition routine to help you feel prepared and focused before you arrive at the event. It is important that you create a clear plan so that you know which triggers you will use and when to help you get into your performance zone and stay there so you are able to perform at your best throughout all 3 phases. You will find it helpful to mentally rehearse using these triggers, and you can even incorporate this into your practise at home so you remember exactly when to use them at events.

When you use this strategy in combination with the other mindset strategies, you will suddenly find that your performance is lifted up a level and you feel much more confident in your ability to produce your best performance at events. By using the 4 free bonuses provided with this book to work out which strategies are most important for you, and to work out which mindset strategies to use at each stage of the competition, you will be able to see just how this particular strategy fits in with the others. If you have not already registered to get your 4 free bonuses, simply go to www.Transform PressureToPower.com to get them now.

ACTION

Complete steps 1 to 3 in the Get Trigger Power section of this chapter.

NOTE ON TRIGGER CREATION

This chapter has focused on using existing triggers derived from your life experience to help you perform at your best at events. If you want to create brand new triggers, be aware that this is a mechanical process that requires your brain to learn to associate something with a feeling. You'll need to establish a new connection between something and a behaviour. This can take time and it is best done with the help of a professional, qualified in neuro-linguistic programming (NLP) or sports psychology.

PERCEPTION IS KING

The reason I am so passionate about encouraging you to use triggers and ignore the cynics who believe that your triggers are just superstitions is because perception rules. Perception is reality. Whatever you believe helps you to perform at your best will help you. It doesn't matter if other people think you are crazy or superstitious; all that matters is that it works for you. If you have time, I encourage you to Google "placebo effect" and read all about amazing studies of how our ability to believe in something allows us to overcome obstacles and achieve truly outstanding things.

Here's just one example. Whilst treating wounded American soldiers during World War II, a doctor called Henry Beecher faced a dilemma when his supply of the painkiller morphine ran out. Medical supplies were in short supply so with no option to get any more morphine at short notice, Henry made a judgement call. He decided to inject soldiers with saline solution (salt water) and told the soldiers they were being injected with morphine. An amazing 40% of the soldiers reported that the saline injection eased their pain. This is just one example of how powerful our perception really is because it can change our reality!

That's why I encourage you to be creative and give yourself permission to believe in your triggers and ignore the cynics. Rational thinking absolutely has its place in the world and without it we wouldn't have a structured, ordered society. Belief elevates you to a new level of performance power and, once you discover that, you won't want to go back. It will open your eyes to possibilities you didn't see before. It's something I've only discovered in the last few years since my accident, and I'm so grateful for that accident because without it, I wouldn't have been able to transform my life and achieve incredible things, like writing this book!

FINAL THOUGHTS...

Practise and preparation are absolutely key. To get maximum benefit from this book, it's really important that you commit to taking action and practising these strategies. I recommend you use the Mindset Improvement Plan, which is one of the 4 free bonuses that comes with this book, to map out the steps you will take to implement the strategies. If you haven't already registered for these free gifts, simply go to www.TransformPressureToPower.com and enter your details for access.

The mindset strategies I've outlined in this book compliment the technical preparation and practise you do with your instructor or technical coach. These strategies do not replace technical preparation and practise! If you're unprepared for the challenge of an upcoming event, your emotions will overwhelm you and you will find it difficult to control them. In this situation, the fix is not a mindset strategy; it's technical practise. When you are underprepared and you get anxious it's because you know you are not prepared and therefore unlikely to succeed. If you are unsure or worried about any aspect of your technical practise or preparation before an event, you must discuss this with your instructor. Be as specific as possible when you explain what you are experiencing so your instructor understands exactly what is happening and can help you find a solution.

So, did you take the actions I gave you in each chapter of this book? When you accurately and consistently apply the strategies in this book I am 100% confident you will improve your competition performance, and you may be pleasantly surprised by the results you achieve. Even just applying one strategy consistently will improve your performance and if you used my mindset strategy questionnaires, which is one of the free gifts you get when you register at www.TransformPressureTo Power.com to identify the highest priority strategy for you and just focus on implementing that, I know you'll achieve better results.

This book provides you with a solid foundation of tools and techniques that will help you to build a winning mindset. It really is just a small proportion of the tools and techniques I use to help riders just like you, which is why I deliver group workshops and conduct individual coaching sessions. It would not be possible to document everything in a book without overloading you with information, which is why I've focused on giving you the essential starting points for building a winning mindset so you can get going with strengthening your mental game and improving your performance at competitions. The next step after this book is to further tailor these strategies to help you get from where you are now to where you want to be with your eventing performances. The best way to do this is to have coaching sessions with me. So if you've enjoyed my book and want to continue the coaching conversation with me, I'd love to hear from you. You can get in touch with me via my website or email Helen@TransformPressureToPower.com

Stay calm and focused under pressure!

48819006R00074

Made in the USA
Charleston, SC
11 November 2015